THE

LEATHERWORKING

HANDBOOK

THE
LEATHERWORKING
HANDBOOK

A PRACTICAL ILLUSTRATED SOURCEBOOK
OF TECHNIQUES AND PROJECTS

VALERIE MICHAEL

CASSELL

To my mother and father

A CASSELL BOOK

First published in the UK
1993 by Cassell
Wellington House
125 Strand
WC2 0BB

Distributed in the United States
by Sterling Publishing Co., Inc.
387 Park Avenue South, New York, NY 10016–8810

Distributed in Australia
by Capricorn Link (Australia) Pty Ltd
2/13 Carrington Road, Castle Hill, NSW 2154

British Library Cataloguing-in-Publication Data.
A catalogue record for this book is available from the British Library.

ISBN 0–304–34511–3

Typeset by Columns of Reading
Printed and bound in China by
Dah Hua Printing Co

CONTENTS

Acknowledgements 6
Introduction 7

PART ONE

1. WHAT IS LEATHER? 10
Tanning
Cow hide
Skins

2. THE WORKSHOP 14
Tools for leatherworking
Tool preparation and
maintenance

3. MATERIALS 22
Threads
Dyes
Leather dressings and polishes
Adhesives
Linings
Reinforcements

4. METAL FITTINGS 25
Buckles
Locks
Stud fastenings
Rings
Preparing metal fittings

PART TWO

5. DESIGNING AND PATTERN
MAKING 28
The design brief
Cutting out

6. DYEING AND FINISHING 31
Dyeing
Finishing

7. EDGE FINISHING 34
Cut-edge finishing
Turned-edge finishing
Bound-edge finishing
Piped seams

8. PARING OR SKIVING,
SPLITTING AND
CHANNELLING 40
Paring or skiving
Splitting
Channelling

9. GLUING 44

10. HAND STITCHING 46
Saddle stitch
Box stitch
Butt stitch
Back stitch

11. GUSSETS 57
One-piece cut-edged gusset
Three-piece cut-edged gusset
U-shaped cut-edged gusset
U-shaped bound-edged gusset

12. POCKETS 60
Flat pockets
Gusseted pockets
Hanging pockets

13. ATTACHING LOCKS,
BUCKLES AND STUDS 62
Locks
Buckles
Studs

14. STRAPS AND HANDLES 68
Shoulder straps
Handles

15. MOULDING AND SURFACE
DECORATION 72
Moulding
Surface Decoration

PART THREE

16. BEGINNERS' PROJECTS 78
Hide belt
Purse
Mask

17. INTERMEDIATE PROJECTS 86
Wallet and passport holder
Folding-top bag
Small briefcase

18. ADVANCED PROJECTS 96
Box bag
Moulded shoulder bag
Quilted belt
Large shoulder bag

Glossary 116
Suppliers 117
Useful Addresses 120
Courses 121
Museums to Visit 122
Further Reading 123
Index 125

ACKNOWLEDGEMENTS

I would like to thank everyone who has given me practical and moral support during the writing of this book. I particularly thank Neil MacGregor for reading the manuscript to make sure it made sense and for offering positive suggestions to improve it. I am also grateful to Brian Ainley for his patience in taking all the black and white photographs; to Lynne Castell for her care and accuracy in converting my sketches into clear line drawings; and to Martin Green for taking most of the colour photographs. Special thanks to Duncan for looking after himself when I needed to write.

INTRODUCTION

This book has been written to provide a practical guide for those who wish to make hand-stitched leather goods. The information and advice contained in these pages are based on 20 years of experience as a self-employed designer and maker, and I hope that they will inspire you to take up this absorbing craft or, if you have already begun to work with leather, that it will encourage you to make some more unusual and adventurous items.

The book is divided into three main parts, and there are lists of suppliers and useful books at the back. Part 1 describes the materials and tools you will need. The chapters in this section explain how leather is made, particularly vegetable tanned leather, how it is sold and how it can be used. The other materials you will need are also described. The workshop plan is an idealized layout – the sort of room I would like if I was just starting out. The list of leatherworking tools should help you to identify the most useful hand tools to buy at the beginning, and it also suggests those you can add to your range as the need and opportunity arises.

Part 2 is the resource section. It is full of illustrated descriptions of how to work with vegetable tanned leathers, with constructional ideas for you to refer to when you make your own designs. If you forget about speed and concentrate on mastering the techniques, the results may surprise you. There are always new ideas to explore, so be prepared to experiment with unusual leathers, colours and shapes.

Part 3 contains ten projects for you to make. These are divided into three groups. The first three projects are for beginners, but I hope that they will also be valuable to those with some experience. They have been designed to introduce beginners to the first techniques that need to be learned – pattern making, cutting out, cut-edge finishing, skiving, stitching and simple moulding. Next are three intermediate projects. These introduce paring skills, fixing studs and locks, attaching simple straps and handles, and making a pocket and gusset. The final four projects should be attempted only after you have gained some experience of working with leather, and each introduces a different range of skills.

Obtaining reliable supplies of good quality raw materials is always a problem for students, and it does not get much easier for the professional leatherworker either! This is why I have included such a long list of suppliers, coded to indicate the nature of their business – manufacturer, retailer and so on – and whether they supply small quantities. If a supplier will deal only in large amounts, try to find someone else with whom you can share an order – obtaining good quality leather and fittings is worth extra trouble and expense.

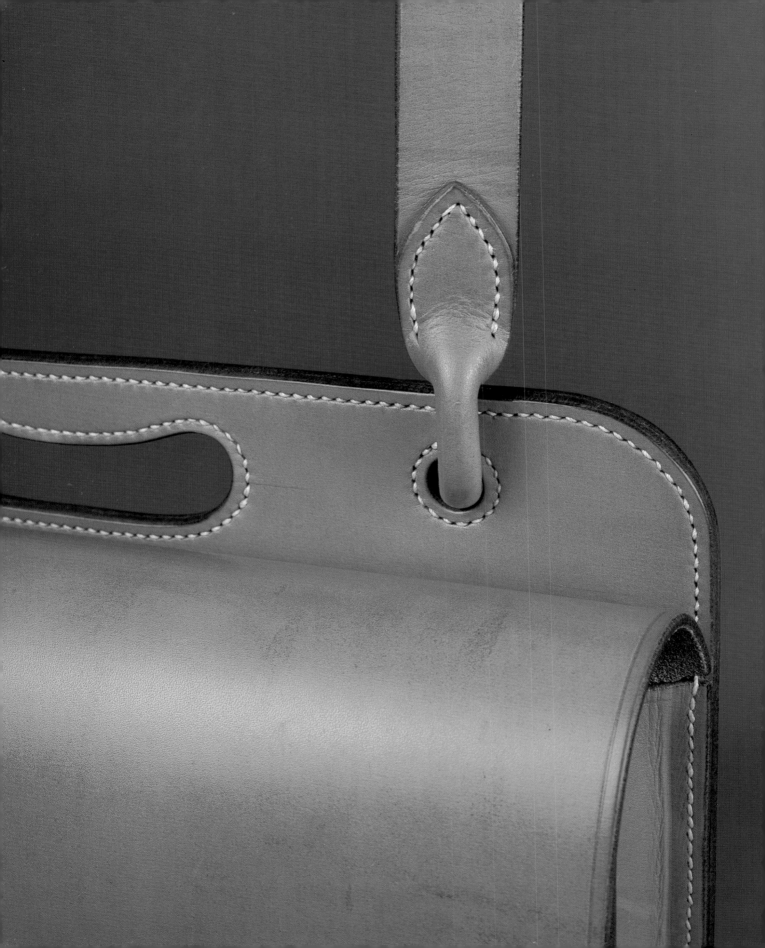

PART I

1

WHAT IS LEATHER?

Leather is not simply the skin of a dead animal; it is a material made by a tanner. Once an animal has been killed for food, the skin becomes a waste product, which could be thrown away and allowed to decompose. Instead, it is transformed into a flexible, tactile material with a multitude of uses.

Leatherworkers have long been aware of the special nature of leather, but it was not until the coming of microscopy that the underlying structure of leather was discovered and its secret revealed. From the leatherworker's point of view, the most important part of an animal skin is the corium (Fig. 1). The corium consists mainly of the protein collagen, the fibres of which are grouped together into 'bundles'. It is the three-dimensional interweaving of these bundles of fibres throughout the thickness of the skin

FIG. 1 *A highly magnified cross-section of a piece of skin.*

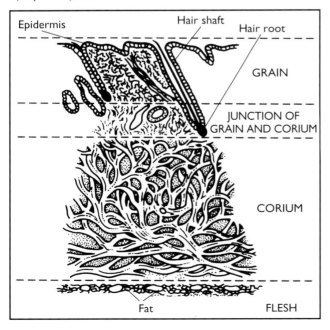

that gives leather its unique structure and adaptability. The largest bundles are found in the middle of the corium, and the fibres become finer and more closely woven towards the surface of the grain. It is the organization of the bundles of fibres and their ability to move in response to stresses and strains that give leather its characteristics – its flexibility, strength, elasticity, malleability and ability to breathe. By studying the structure of the fibres, leather chemists have discovered how to affect the angle at which the fibres are woven and so to produce a range of leathers suited to a variety of specific needs.

TANNING

Tanning can be described as the production from animal skin of a chemically and biologically stable material by a process that leaves the original fibre structure more or less intact. It is a process that transforms animal skin, which is a highly complex product of nature, into a sophisticated material with countless uses.

Before tanning can begin, hides and skins have to be modified by a series of pre-tanning operations. These include the removal of the hair and epidermis from the top, a process known as liming, and the removal of the layer of flesh from underneath, which is known as fleshing. It is the middle layer, the corium, that is left and that becomes leather.

Tanning methods using smoke, animal and fish oils, and alum salts (known as tawing), are still practised throughout the world on a small scale. The two main methods of tanning in use today, however, are chrome tanning and vegetable tanning.

CHROME TANNING

Chrome tanning was developed towards the end of the nineteenth century. Hides and skins are tumbled in drums containing solutions of chromium salts and other special chemicals until tanning is complete. It can take as little as a few hours to tan some skins and one day to tan a cow hide. Most of the leather used for shoes, clothing and upholstery is now produced by this method.

Chrome leathers are characterized by their light weight and high tensile strength. They are also made waterproof by fat liquoring. Recent advances in chrome tanning have meant that leathers that drape like fabric can be produced in fabulous colours. Chrome leathers cannot successfully be used for hand working using the methods described in this book, however, because they are too soft and stretchy. They were developed for the speed of machinery and mass-production methods.

VEGETABLE TANNING

In vegetable tanning a solution known as a liquor is made from an infusion of ground tree bark, twigs, leaves and water. The skins or hides are immersed in this liquor, either suspended in pits or tumbled in drums, until tanning is completed. The chemical composition of this tanning liquor has to be carefully monitored by the tanner to produce leather of consistent quality. Some of the most widely used vegetable tanning materials are the barks of oak, hemlock, mangrove, mallet (a kind of eucalyptus), birch, larch and pine, and extracts from chestnut wood, mimosa,

quebracho (a South American tree), myrobalans (the fruit of an Indian tree), valonia (the acorn–cup of the Levantine oak) and sumach leaves and twigs. The choice of tanning material determines not only the time required for the process but also the characteristics and colour of the leather – its density, flexibility and the ease with which it can be cut.

The traditional method of vegetable tanning is in pits. Hides are suspended or laid flat in a series of pits containing tanning liquors. These are arranged so that initially the hide comes into contact with weak liquors, and then gradually, as its fibres become tanned, it is exposed to stronger, more concentrated solutions until tanning is complete. This process can take up to a year for oak bark sole leather or three months for 3mm ($1/8$in/8oz) bag leather. The hides and tanning liquor move in opposite directions through the tannery (Fig. 2). As the strong tanning liquor in the final pit weakens, it is pumped from pit to pit down the yard until it reaches the first pit, its strength gradually reducing.

The precious weak tanning liquor in the first pit is non-astringent, and it lightly tans and colours the hides. It is highly acidic, which helps tannin to penetrate by plumping up the fibres. Although it slows down the tanning process, it permits the tan to be fixed rapidly, and this results in a firmer leather. If the tanning liquors in the first pits are too strong, the surface of the hide tans too soon and the tanning is uneven, resulting in 'case hardening' and cracking.

FIG. 2 *Hides and tanning liquor moving in opposite directions through the tannery.*

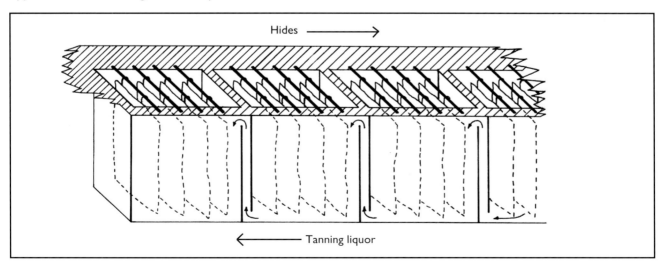

Most vegetable tanned skins and an increasing amount of hide are now tanned in large drums. Drum tanning gives much quicker results, but the mechanical action of the drum can damage the grain surface of hide. Leather tanned by this method tends to be of a lighter weight and more 'mellow' (softer) than pit-tanned leather.

Each of the different tanning methods and materials produces leather with different characteristics. The techniques and projects described in this book exploit the qualities and creative potential of vegetable tanned leathers. The processes described in the following chapters have been developed by working with vegetable tanned leathers, and the projects described and illustrated in Part 3 have been designed to use these leathers. The appeal of vegetable tanned leather is hard to define – its smell, how it feels when you run your fingers over its surface, the way it flexes and changes colour with time and use. There is no other material like it!

COW HIDE

The leather you will use most often is cow hide. The best quality is described as full grain, which means that the surface has not been 'corrected'. All leather has surface marks – they add to its character – and open cuts, deep scratches and holes can be avoided during cutting out. However, full grain hide is becoming more difficult to find because of the practice of 'buffing' off the grain surface to remove any

LEATHER THICKNESS CONVERSION CHART

Millimetre	Inch	Ounce*	Iron**
0.4	$1/64$	1	$3/4$
0.8	$1/32$	2	$1 1/2$
1.2	$3/64$	3	$2 1/4$
1.6	$1/16$	4	3
2.0	$5/64$	5	$3 3/4$
2.4	$3/32$	6	$4 1/2$
2.8	$7/64$	7	$5 1/4$
3.2	$1/8$	8	6
3.6	$9/64$	9	$6 3/4$
4.0	$5/32$	10	$7 1/2$

* In the US leather is measured in ounces.
** In shoe-making sole leather is measured in units of irons.

imperfections. Unfortunately, buffing dulls and flattens the leather's surface and causes problems with dyeing.

Hide can be bought in a natural condition, when it is known as russet, or pre-dyed and ready to use. When you buy leather, you should always try to visit the supplier yourself rather than risk being sent something from the bottom of the pile. Once the supplier

SECTIONS OF COW HIDE

Sections of a hide	Characteristics	Thickness in mm and possible use					
		1.5	2	2.5	3	3.5	4
Butt	The best and most expensive area; strong, tight fibre structure		Bags	Cases Boxes	Belts		
Back	The butt area plus the shoulder		Bags	Boxes	Belts		
Shoulder	Looser and more uneven fibre structure than butt; interesting growth pattern on surface		Bags	Cases Boxes			
Side	A half hide	Masks	Bags	Cases	Boxes		
Belly	Loose fibre structure, uneven thickness, stretchy	Masks and moulding					

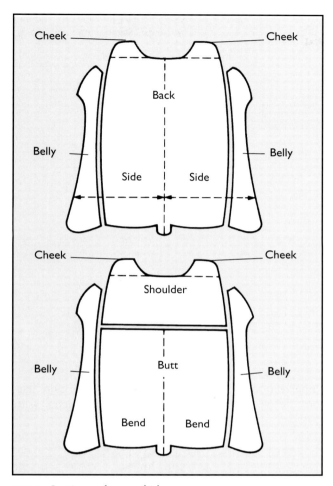

FIG. 3 *Sections of a cow hide.*

knows that your standards are high you can buy by mail order, but always send back poor quality leather. If you can see that it is dry and scratched, the person who sent it certainly knew it was too. (Leather suppliers are listed on page 117.)

Unless you need a very large area – whole hides can measure up to 5.2 square metres (56 square feet) – you will usually buy cow hide by the section or piece (Fig. 3).

Shoulders are ideal for novice leatherworkers because it is possible to achieve good results without having to spend a fortune. Natural russet is inexpensive but needs dyeing and finishing in the workshop. The best hides tend to be selected for saddlery and harness work, and they are dyed, oiled and coated with tallow. If you use saddlery leather for leather goods, therefore, you will have to rub the surface with a soft cloth. Good quality pre-dyed case or bag hide is ideal if you can find it, but belly, although cheap, is useful only for experiments or for moulded work.

SKINS

The word skin is used for leather from small animals. Skins are usually sold whole, by the square foot. They are thinner than hide, so are much lighter in weight. Skins are mainly used for small leather goods, pockets and linings or are combined with hide for large bags and cases.

TYPES AND CHARACTERISTICS OF SKINS

Type	Characteristics	Thickness in mm	Uses
Calf	Silky, firm surface and a tight fibre structure; sometimes has an embossed grain pattern	0.5–1.5	Quilted bags and belts; wallets and purses; linings and pockets
Pig	Distinctive triple-hair grain markings; it is very strong and hard wearing	0.5–1.5	Bags, belts, wallets, purses and brief cases; linings and pockets
Goat	A pronounced grain and loose fibre structure; it is easy to pare	1.0–1.5	Bags, purses, wallets and bookbindings
Kid	Usually has a glazed surface; a delicate, lightweight leather	0.3–0.8	Small bags and belts; good for linings
Sheep	Loose-fibred with a dull grain; dyes easily	1.0–1.5	Leather aprons, bellows; skivers used for box covering and restoration

2

THE WORKSHOP

It is essential that you have a place to work. A light, well-ventilated workshop is ideal, but to begin with you will be able to manage with just a workbench (Fig. 4). This should be about waist high and have a foot rail, and should be positioned in front of a window. You will need a stool to sit on. Arrange your tools around the edge so that they are within easy reach. If possible, have some shelves for storing leather and patterns under the bench and to the sides, and remember that you will also need drawers and shelves for your threads, needles and so on. When you need to cut out pieces of leather, lay a thick board on the floor.

FIG. 4 *The workbench.*

If you want to earn your living from making leather goods, you will find it essential to organize a workshop (Fig. 5). A good size would be a room 5 metres (about 16ft) square, with natural daylight coming in from two sides. A large table for cutting out, placed in the centre of the room, will also enable you to examine the leather thoroughly when patterns are being positioned. If possible, incorporate a cutting-board into the table's surface. The area underneath can be used to store leather, patterns and scraps. Workbenches for making up, dyeing, polishing and metalworking can be arranged around the walls. Benches should be at least 75cm (30in) wide and between 75cm and 1 metre (30–36in) high, depending on your height. Have plenty of shelves and cupboards for keeping metal fittings, threads, dyes, polishes and finished work. Running water, a kettle and a telephone would complete the workshop's facilities.

TOOLS FOR LEATHERWORKING

To begin with, you will be able to manage with a few essential tools (Fig. 6), but as your work progresses you will find that a wider range of tools will both save time and give better results (Fig. 7). The list of hand tools that follows briefly describes each tool and explains its use. Those marked with an asterisk (*) are essential, and you will need them before you can start to work with leather.

Awl*
An awl blade is used to pierce the holes before hand stitching can be carried out. Awls are available in sizes ranging from 32 to 90mm ($1^{1}/_{4}$–$3^{1}/_{2}$in). For most work you will find that a 57mm ($2^{1}/_{4}$in) blade will be suitable. The blades are diamond shaped, tapering to a sharp point that penetrates leather easily.

FIG. 5 *The workshop.*

A scratch awl has a round, tapered blade and is used to mark around patterns before cutting out.

Awl handles are sold separately, and the best are made from one of the hardwoods. Choose a shape that fits comfortably into your hand. Make sure that the tapered end is narrow, or the ferule (the metal band encircling the taper) will damage the leather when you are stitching fine work. To set an awl blade in a handle see pages 20–1.

Bone folder*

A smooth, polished piece of bone between 12.5 and 20cm (5–8in) long, of the kind familiar to book-binders, is used for 'boning down' seams and turning edges.

Bulldog clips*

These clips are available from stationers. Cover the jaws with thin leather and use them for holding edges together when you are gluing.

Burnisher

A smooth, shaped piece of boxwood, a burnisher is used to seal and burnish the grain surface of natural leathers.

Clam*

Known also as clamps, clams are essential for hand stitching. The best are made from a hardwood such

as ash, beech or oak. When you are stitching, the clam holds the work, leaving your hands free to hold the awl and needles. It is held between your knees.

Compass/dividers*

These are used to mark guidelines for stitching and creasing.

Creaser*

When it is heated and pressed firmly into the surface of leather, the creaser leaves a thin, decorative line. It is mainly used close to edges or on lapped joints to hide seams. The single creaser is most useful.

Cutting-board

A professional cutting-board made of square wooden blocks, preferably lime, which are glued together with the end grain forming the cutting surface, will not blunt your knife. It can be let into the top of your cutting table and, when it is worn, the surface can be scraped smooth and dressed with linseed oil.

Edge beveller*

Also known as an edge shave, an edge beveller is used to round off the edges of thick leathers ready for bur-nishing. They are available with a flat back or with a concave back (when they are known as hollow ground), in sizes 1–8. For most work, sizes 1–3 are adequate.

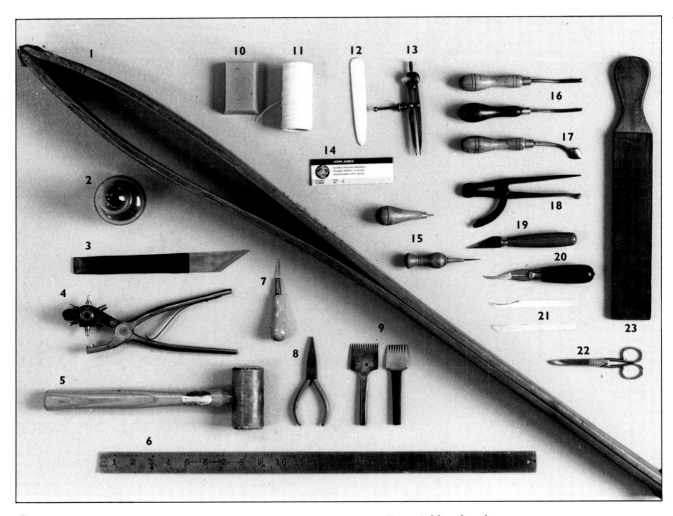

FIG. 6 **Essential hand tools**

1 *clam*
2 *spirit lamp*
3 *paring knife*
4 *six-way revolving punch*
5 *hide hammer*
6 *steel rule*
7 *scratch awl*
8 *flat-nosed pliers*
9 *pricking irons, numbers 7 and 8*
10 *beeswax*
11 *linen thread*
12 *bone folder*
13 *dividers*
14 *harness needles*
15 *stitching awls*
16 *edge bevellers*
17 *single creaser*
18 *compass race*
19 *knife*
20 *clicking knife*
21 *spare blades for clicking knife*
22 *scissors*
23 *strop*

G-cramps

These woodworkers' tools are useful for securing the paring machine to the workbench and for moulding.

Hammer*

Hide or wooden hammers should be used to strike metal tools because they do not damage the tool shank. Shoemaker's and bookbinder's hammers have large, flattened, circular heads, and they are ideal for flattening seams and turned edges.

Knives*

Your choice of knife will depend on the thickness of leather to be cut, the shape of the pattern pieces and the size of hand. For most work you will find that a shoemaker's knife with a shortened blade is easy to use and to sharpen. When you are cutting out curved or awkward shaped pieces, a 'clicking knife' with a

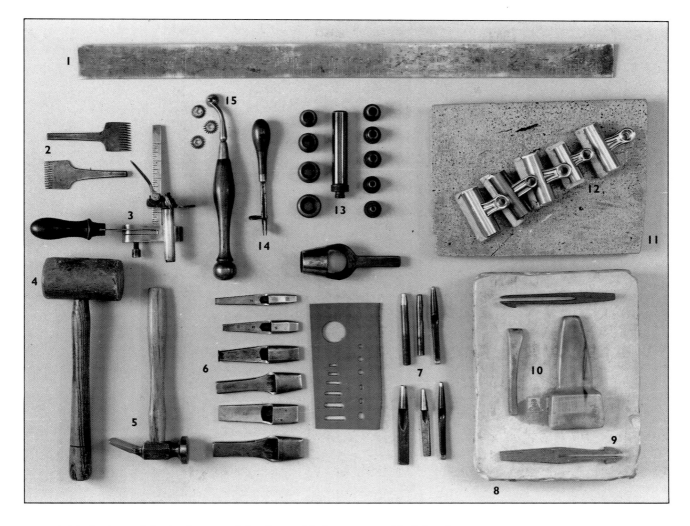

FIG. 7 **Useful tools**
1 *heavy steel rule*
2 *pricking irons, numbers 9 and 10*
3 *plough gauge*
4 *heavy wooden mallet*
5 *shoemaker's hammer*
6 *range of crew punches*
7 *range of oval and round punches*
8 *litho stone*
9 *loop clamp*
10 *boxwood burnishers*
11 *cork block*
12 *leather-covered bulldog clips*
13 *range of round punches*
14 *small screw crease*
15 *pricking wheels and carriage*

curved blade is useful. A sharpened hacksaw blade also makes a good knife, but do take care to wrap up the part of the blade you are going to hold.

Needles*

Until recently, the blunt, egg-eyed harness needles used for hand stitching were available in 11 sizes, but now the range has been reduced to seven. Small stocks of sizes 5 and 6 may be found in odd places but you can start with size 4, which will be suitable for general work.

Paring knife*

You will need a steep-angled knife, with a long, bevelled cutting edge on one side and a completely flat back. This is used to reduce the thickness of leather along edges.

FIG. 8 *A JB4 leather paring machine.*

FIG. 9 *A detail of a paring machine, showing the anvil, wing nut adjusting screw and position of the razor blade.*

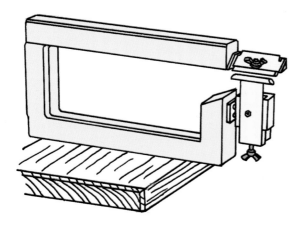

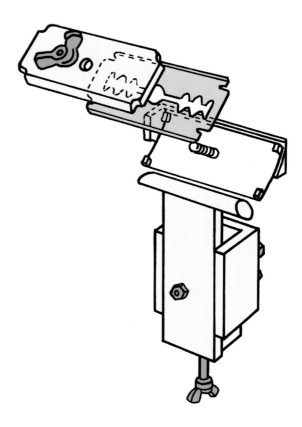

Paring machine

This simple-to-use, bench-mounted machine (Fig. 8) was designed by a bookbinder to pare flat areas of leather to an even thickness or to make a bevelled pare along edges. It uses a standard double-sided razor blade, positioned over an anvil (Fig. 9), and you can adjust the anvil up or down to set the depth of cut or tilt it to achieve a bevelled pare.

Paring stone

An oblong slab of soft stone used in lithographic printing, known as a litho stone, is ideal for paring because it will not blunt your knife. It has a smooth, polished surface, which can be sanded flat. If you cannot obtain a litho stone, a thick piece of plate glass or marble will do instead.

Pliers*

You will need flat-nosed engineer's or saddler's pliers to pull through stubborn needles and to grip leather at the beginning of a cut made with a plough gauge or splitting machine.

Plough gauge

A plough gauge is used for cutting belts and straps. The width of strap is determined by sliding a fence along a graduated gauge, and the strap is cut by pushing the knife, which is mounted to the right of the gauge, parallel to the edge of the leather.

Press

A heavy cast iron bench press, familiar to bookbinders as a nipping press, is used for exerting pressure over large areas. It is useful when you are attaching glued linings and for embossing.

Pricking iron*

This steel tool is used to mark the position of stitches, but it is not designed to penetrate the leather completely. Each tooth is ground so that it has a chisel-shaped head at an angle of about 45 degrees to the horizontal. The number of teeth in each iron is determined by the width of the iron and the number of stitches to the inch – for example, 1in wide number 7 has eight teeth, a number 8 has nine teeth and so on. They are available in sizes (that is, number of stitches to the inch) 4–12.

Pricking wheel

A small steel wheel mounted in a frame is used to mark stitches in the same way as a pricking iron. It is useful for making leather-covered buckles.

Punches

Punches are tubular steel tools for cutting holes. An oval hole in a strap helps the tongue lie flat and reduces the strain. Crew punches cut neat slots for buckles and straps.

Race*

A race is a grooving tool with a U- or V-shaped cutter for removing a thin channel of leather. It is used on the flesh side to make it easier to form a sharp bend or on the grain surface to sink stitches.

Revolving punch plier*

Six round punches, ranging in size from 1.6mm to 6.4mm ($^1/_{16}$–$^1/_4$in), are mounted in a revolving head. Those made of solid forged steel are best.

Scissors*

Sharpening stone*

Japanese water stones are very fast-cutting but soft. Combination oil stones have a coarse and a fine layer joined together. Woodworking tool suppliers will stock a range.

Spirit lamp*

The kind of lamp that burns on methylated spirit is used to heat creasing tools.

Splitting machine

A cast iron frame with a horizontally fixed steel blade is used to reduce the thickness of leather straps or gussets. The machines are available in blade sizes 128mm (5in), 153mm (6in) and 204mm (8in), but unless the blade is kept very sharp, it is difficult to pull through a width greater than 10cm (4in).

Straight edge or ruler*

You will need a steel rule, at least 2mm ($^1/_{16}$in) thick.

Strop*

A flat piece of wood with a layer of leather, flesh side up and impregnated with emery paste, glued to one side, is essential for keeping knives sharp.

TOOL PREPARATION AND MAINTENANCE

New knives and awl blades always need sharpening and polishing before they can be used. A sharpening kit should consist of:

- a combination oil stone or Japanese water stone (4000 grit)
- a strop
- medium and fine emery papers
- emery paste
- jeweller's rouge

TO MAKE A STROP

Cut a 10mm ($^1/_2$in) piece of plywood about 350 × 65mm ($13^3/_4$ × $2^1/_2$in) and shape one end into a simple handle. Glue some hide, grain side down, to one side and rub fine emery paste, the kind used by engineers, into the leather with some oil. If you wish, glue another piece of leather to the underside and impregnate this with jeweller's rouge. This will give a high polish to knife and awl blades.

SHARPENING KNIVES

Look at the bevelled angle each side of the knife blade before you attempt to sharpen it. These angles must be maintained. Lay the flat area of one side of the knife on the stone and gently tilt it until you feel the bevel come into contact with the stone. Make sure that there is water or oil on the surface of the stone, then move the blade forwards and backwards (Fig. 10) until a slight 'burr' can be seen running along the edge of the blade. This thin shaving of metal indicates that the blade can be turned over and the process repeated on the other side. The 'burr' will change direction when this side of the blade has been sharpened enough. The burr can be removed when the blade is polished on the strop. Observation and experience are the only ways to learn how to sharpen and maintain the edges of your knives. If you persevere, cutting out with a sharp knife will be easier and safer and the results will be more accurate. Keep your newly sharpened knife in condition by stropping it often and make a cover to protect it.

Your paring knife can be sharpened in a similar way, except that there is a bevel on only one side of the blade (Fig. 11). The flat side must be completely flat if the knife is to work properly. Remove the burr

FIG. 10 *Sharpening a cutting knife on a water stone.*

FIG. 11 (right) *Sharpening a paring knife on a water stone.*

by drawing the flat of the blade gently over the strop. The blade of a plough gauge usually has one long and one short bevel. Be sure to maintain the long bevel or the leather will 'pull away' from the fence when you cut a strap.

SHARPENING EDGE BEVELLERS

A blunt edge beveller leaves a rough edge, which makes burnishing more difficult. Rub the underside of a flat beveller on a fine sharpening stone until you have a 'burr', which can be removed with a piece of fine emery paper, folded and drawn through the groove on the top. Use a small slip stone to reshape the underside of a hollow-ground beveller.

SETTING AN AWL BLADE

Use two copper coins to hold the blade in a vice with the shank pointing up (Fig. 12). Make sure it is vertical by looking at it from the front and from the sides. Gently tap the handle on to the blade (Fig. 13). Leave at least 2cm ($^3/_4$in) of blade protruding from the handle (Fig. 14) and make sure it is set straight. Each facet of the blade must be polished on fine emery paper and finished on the strop. If you take the trouble to prepare your awls in this way, they will pierce the leather easily and make stitching more enjoyable and less tiring.

FIG. 12 *An awl blade ready to set in a handle with the aid of two copper coins. A finished awl.*

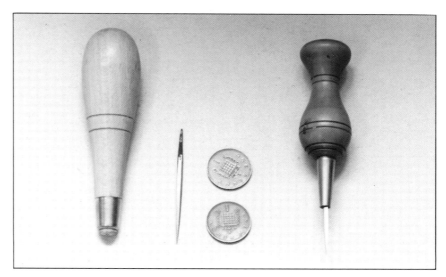

FIG. 13 (below) *Gently tapping the handle on to the awl blade.*

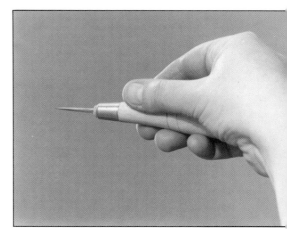

FIG. 14 *Blade set and ready for polishing.*

3

MATERIALS

THREADS

You should use the best quality linen thread for most hand-stitched work. Cotton threads are too weak, and synthetic polyester threads, although strong, are difficult to tension because they stretch. Pure silk thread is strong enough to make wallets or small bags, and it is ideal for quilting. It should be equivalent to a size 40 linen thread (colour photograph 1).

The common sizes of linen threads are 18 (3-, 4-, 5- and 6-cords), 25 (3-cord), 30 (3-cord), 35 (3-cord) and 40 (3-cord). They are sold in reels of 25gm, 50gm or 250gm in black, brown, white and yellow.

To make threads with more cords or strands, you can buy a continuous length of linen, known as 'twist', and use this to roll together the required number of

1 *Linen and silk threads with awls,*
beeswax and harness needles.

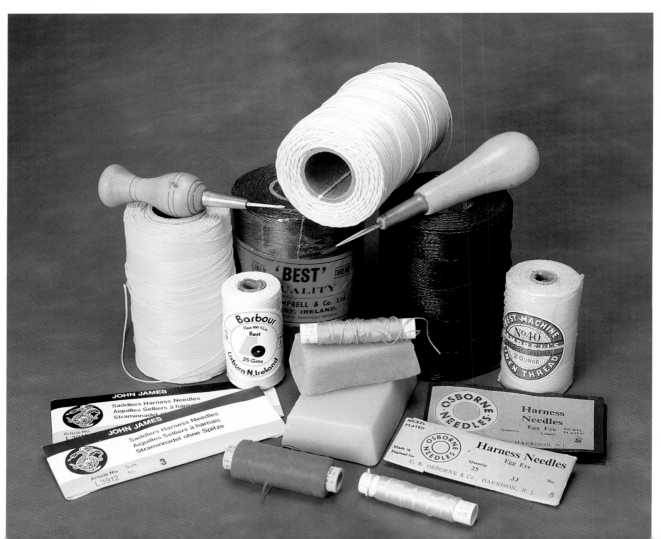

2 Leather dyes.

strands into lengths of thread, which are tapered at each end and ready for threading your needles.

The choice of thread size is determined by the number of stitches to the inch and the thickness of the leather. Before you begin stitching, coat the threads with a layer of beeswax to protect them. Beeswax is sold in small blocks and is available from most craft shops.

DYES

Dyes can be water- or spirit-based (colour photograph 2). They are used to colour the edges of pre-dyed leather before burnishing or to colour large areas of natural leather. They do not obscure the grain surface because they penetrate the leather. Acrylic dyes are really paints that lie on the surface of the leather. They are available in bright colours but should be used for decorative effects rather than all-over colouring.

LEATHER DRESSINGS AND POLISHES

If leather has been dyed or if you want a natural finish, it will need 'feeding' and polishing (colour photograph 3, and chart on page 24). Pre-dyed leather will already have been treated with a fat liquor, oil or tallow by the currier, and it should not need further treatment.

ADHESIVES

Adhesives (glues and cements) are used to bond surfaces together permanently or to tack them temporarily prior to stitching (colour photograph 4). When you are working with leather, the qualities

3 Leather polishes and finishes.

4 Rubber solution, gum used for edge burnishing and PVA adhesive.

DRESSINGS AND POLISHES

Pliantene	Also called British Museum Leather Dressing, it was developed to treat old leather bookbindings. It is made from a combination of beeswax, cedar wood oil and lanolin dissolved in hexane. It penetrates well and smells good. As well as lubricating dry leather it imparts a soft shine. Highly recommended.
4–Way Care	A dressing and lubricant that penetrates dry leather without leaving a trace on the surface. Can be applied before dyeing to help with dye penetration.
Neutral shoe cream	Sold in shoe shops, it is easy to apply and imparts a soft shine.
Saddle soap	Ideal for removing any residue of dye left on the surface after dyeing.
Paper gum	Diluted with water, it is used for burnishing edges.

required of an adhesive are strength or power to unite surfaces, flexibility once dry, ease of application and degree of penetration. The most useful adhesives are PVA adhesive and rubber solution.

PVA ADHESIVE

The ideal all-round adhesive is a PVA leatherworking grade adhesive. It is suitable for gluing in linings and reinforcements; it is easy to apply using a brush or spreader; it is flexible when dry; and it can be thinned with water. PVA adhesive is very useful for holding gussets in position while you stitch, because the edges can later be burnished without leaving an ugly glue line. When it is dry, PVA adhesive is clear, so surfaces need to be bonded while the glue is still white and tacky. If it does dry out, it can be reactivated with water.

RUBBER SOLUTION

This brownish adhesive is made from rubber dissolved in a solvent. It gives off strong fumes, so always use it in a well-ventilated room. The consistency of rubber solution makes it difficult to spread over large areas with a brush unless it is thinned down with the appropriate solvent thinner. It is, however, useful for tacking pieces together in box-stitched work, but take care to prevent it coming into contact with edges that are to be burnished.

LININGS

You should line articles only if there are good reasons for doing so. A lining may be necessary to attach several pockets, to strengthen weak or blemished leather, to cover reinforcements, to provide additional support or to improve the aesthetic appeal of an article.

The lining can be made of leather or fabric. Leather is more durable than fabric, but it is heavier, which is an important consideration when you are designing and making a large bag.

Leathers that are suitable for lining are vegetable tanned calf, kid and pigskin. Sheepskin skivers are often used commercially, but they are weak so can be safely used only for lining items that are likely to receive light wear. Strong natural fabrics such as linen, canvas and silk make sympathetic lining materials.

REINFORCEMENTS

Reinforcements are used to strengthen the outer leather, in part or all over, to add substance, to give rigidity and to give support to straps, handles and seams. If you use good quality leathers of the correct thickness, only the minimum amount of reinforcement will be necessary.

REINFORCING MATERIALS

Leather scraps	Flexible; used to strengthen handles, corners and bases of bags and cases and to support pocket tops and seams.
Grey board	Rigid; used as a foundation for built-up cases and box work.
Vileden	Flexible; an iron-on stiffener, which adds substance to thin leathers; useful for turned-edge work.

4

METAL FITTINGS

In order to close bags and cases and to attach straps or handles you will need to use a variety of metal fittings. Illustrated catalogues from suppliers will give you an idea of the range available and how to identify them, but never be tempted to economize by using cheap buckles or locks. Solid brass looks good, particularly with natural leather colours such as tan and brown, while nickle or silver fittings seem to go with black and blue, but the choice is yours (Fig. 15). Some metal fittings are lacquered by the manufacturer, so if they need working on you will have to remove the lacquer with spirit. Many of the better finished buckles and locks are manufactured in Italy, France, Switzerland and Germany, while UK manufacturers produce a wide range of saddlery related fittings, many of which can be successfully used on leather goods. How to attach most of these fittings is described in Part 2.

BUCKLES

Always use good quality, solid buckles. Pressed and plated buckles will feel light and flimsy in comparison. Some saddlery buckles are suitable for straps and narrow belts; they are simple but strong. Belt buckles

FIG. 15 *Solid brass and split rivets; turn lock and folio lock; two whole buckles and nine half-buckles; round harness rings and D-rings; screw stud and durable dot fastener.*

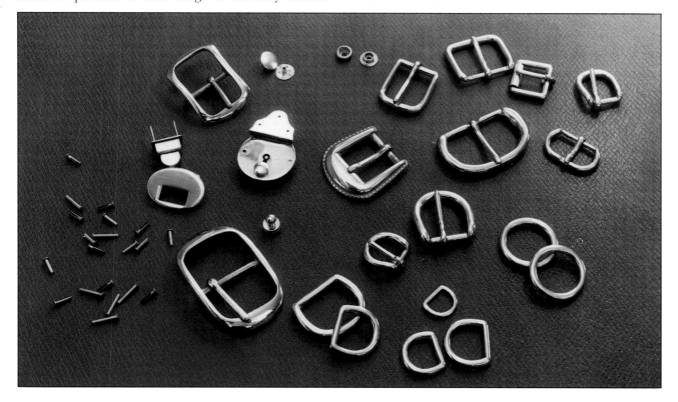

come in shapes and sizes to suit all tastes. It is important that the inside of a buckle is smooth to reduce wear on the edges of the strap. Remove any roughness by filing and clean the buckle with metal polish just before use.

LOCKS

At present only one UK firm makes solid brass locks. The range available includes folio, brief case, attaché case and jewellery case locks. Finding the right size rivets can be a problem, so you may find it necessary to enlarge holes with a round pin-hole file to get rivets to fit. Although it may sound obvious, before you attach a lock always check that it works properly and that the key fits. Turn-locks are useful for closing bags, but stylish, good quality ones are hard to find.

STUD FASTENINGS

Durable dots and press-studs are quick and easy to set and to use. They are rarely made from solid brass, but are more usually brassed or made of nickle-plated steel. Screw studs can be solid brass or nickel or brass-plated. They are the easiest stud to attach as they are held in position by simply screwing the base through the leather into the centre of the stud.

Magnetic studs provide an effective closure for bags and purses that have been lined.

RINGS

Made for the saddlery trade, rings are invaluable for attaching bag straps. They are either D-shaped or round. Sizes range from 12mm to 50mm (1/2–2in).

PREPARING METAL FITTINGS

Brass buckles, rings and locks sometimes need filing to improve their shape or to remove metal that has been left over from the casting process. It is therefore advisable to invest in a small metal working kit (Fig. 16). To begin with you will need:
- a vice
- a few files (second cut)
- a hacksaw
- a box each of medium and fine wire wool
- sheets of medium and fine emery cloth
- a metal hammer
- metal polish
- plenty of old rags

Cover the jaws of the vice to prevent the buckle or fitting being damaged while they are held. (For Suppliers, see pages 117–19.)

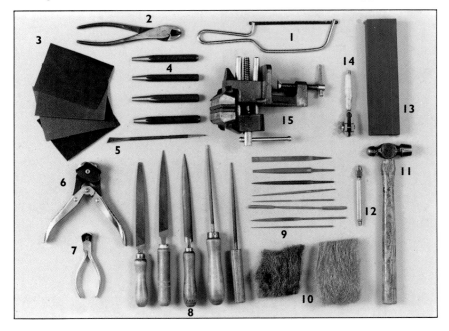

FIG. 16
1 *hacksaw*
2 *flat-backed metal snips*
3 *four grades of emery paper/cloth*
4 *doming punches*
5 *scriber*
6 *large snips*
7 *small snips*
8 *flat, arched and round files*
9 *small files*
10 *wire wool*
11 *metal hammer*
12 *pin vice*
13 *combination oil stone*
14 *small vice*
15 *bench vice*

PART 2

5

DESIGNING AND PATTERN

MAKING

Designing leather goods is not difficult as long as you aim for functional simplicity. You do not even have to be good at drawing provided you understand basic geometry. Established leather goods designers develop a recognizable 'look' or 'style', which evolves because the designer makes clear decisions about the types of leathers he or she likes, the range of work he or she wants to make and the working methods he or she wants to use.

These same choices exist for the student. Design ideas can start life as sketches on scraps of paper. They may be inspired by observing natural forms or perhaps by visiting leather goods shops, or by seeing leather articles in galleries and museums. Simply working with leather, gaining an understanding of its qualities and experimenting with and exploring these qualities will reveal design possibilities.

A blank piece of paper and a vague desire to 'design a bag' is a daunting and unpromising way to start. Begin by setting yourself a design brief.

THE DESIGN BRIEF

'Design a small, lightweight shoulder bag, large enough to carry a purse, a wallet, a slim paperback and keys.' The design brief defines the boundaries within which the designing process will begin. You now need to decide on the type of leather to use – hide or skin – and the approximate size and shape of the bag. Take an off-cut of the leather and handle it to feel the surface and how it flexes. Make some sketches of different bag shapes on pieces of paper until you have an idea that begins to excite your imagination. Among the questions you should ask yourself are: Will the bag have a gusset? If so, what type and size? Will the strap be adjustable? Where and how will it attach to the bag? How will the bag close? Will it have a pocket? What style of construction will it have – cut edged, turned or bound?

When you have made decisions about the basic structure and you have a sketch that you like, your next task is to make an accurate, full-sized drawing so that you can check the proportions and work out the constructional details. Take a large sheet of paper and draw a horizontal line at the bottom. Find the centre of the line and draw a vertical line at a right angle to that point. Mark the proposed height and width, and mark the depth of the flap (if it has one) on the central vertical line. On one half of this outline, draw the shape of your bag, using a compass to make sure that the curves are smooth. Adjust the bag's shape by eye as you draw, making sure that the curves merge imperceptibly with the straight lines. Draw the shape of the flap. Fold the paper along the centre line and use tracing-paper or carbon paper to transfer the bag shape to the other side (Fig. 17). Look critically at your drawing and do not be afraid to adjust the proportions and shapes until it looks 'right'. Now draw a side and back view (Fig. 18). Remember that your drawing is of the finished bag, so you need to visualize it with the gusset, strap and fastenings in place. You will find descriptions and illustrations of different design possibilities throughout this book, and you should look at different bags in leather goods shops to see how they are designed and put together. Once you are satisfied with your drawing, you will have to transfer the design to sheets of thin card in order to make an accurate pattern. As you study the patterns in Part 3 and make some of the simpler projects, you will begin to develop an understanding of how to calculate turning, stitching

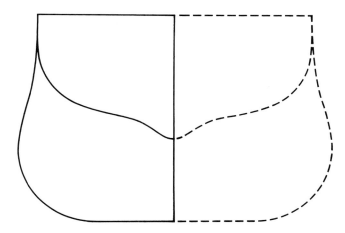

FIG. 17 *The initial drawing of a bag design.*

FIG. 18 *Visualized bag design from the side and back.*

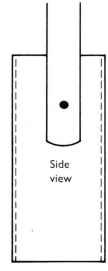

Side view

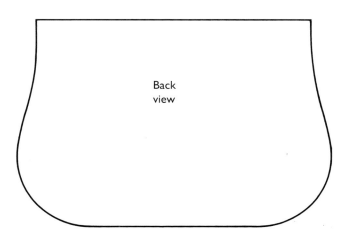

Back view

and gusset allowances and to discover suitable places to position studs and buckles. Remember that your patterns must be accurate. The information they contain is transferred to the leather, and badly cut out, inaccurate patterns will be revealed as soon as you attempt to make any article out of leather.

Before you cut out your new design in leather, it is a good idea to make small mock-ups of constructional details out of the same kind of leather you plan to use for the actual article. It is far better for your confidence to make mistakes or adjustments at this stage rather than when you are half-way through making a project.

CUTTING OUT

Once you are certain that your pattern is absolutely accurate and that the leather you have selected is suitable, it is time to begin the first stage of the making process – cutting out.

Cutting out requires a sharp knife (see Chapter 2), good light and a firm, flat surface. Never be in a hurry or you may make expensive mistakes. Examine the grain surface of the leather you have chosen for scratches, holes and uneven colouring. Highlight any holes or slits on the flesh side so that you can avoid them. When you position the pattern pieces, avoid open scars and damaged areas but remember that leather is a natural material and that some surface marks will be inevitable. The pronounced grain pattern on hide shoulders can add character to an otherwise plain bag.

Always position the pattern pieces from head to tail or from side to side, never diagonally. The best area of a hide or a skin is down the spine and over the rump, so use this for the important pieces of a pattern, such as the front, back and flap of a bag or case. If possible, cut handles, billets and D-ring holders from the butt area; these parts of a bag take a lot of wear and therefore need to be strong. Hide becomes thinner and more loosely fibred towards the belly, so this area is useful for gussets (as long as it is not too stretchy) and for masks, when the loose fibres make moulding easier (see Chapter 15). When you are happy with the position of the pattern pieces, mark clearly around each one with a sharp pencil or, better still, a scratch awl. Hold large pattern pieces in place with masking-tape. Transfer important constructional information – centres, gusset, strap, stud and lock positions, for example – from the pattern to the leather at this stage with the point of the scratch awl. Remove the patterns and begin to cut out.

Keeping the knife upright, cut through the leather by exerting firm, downwards pressure. Make sure that you do not let the knife lean to one side, which is a common problem especially when curves are cut. Use the thumb of the hand in which you are holding your knife as a pivot to balance the blade and keep it upright. Use the other hand to hold the leather down but keep it well away from the knife blade. Whenever possible, cut towards you, not from side to side. Reposition the leather or move yourself around the cutting table so that you can remain comfortable and relaxed. Remember that mistakes happen when you are in a hurry. Strop the knife regularly; a blunt knife is more dangerous than a sharp one because of the extra pressure needed to make a cut. Usually, skins can be cut through with just one knife cut. If the hide is thicker than 2mm (5oz) you may need to make two cuts into the same line before the leather is completely cut through.

Hide belts and straps should be made from firm hide 2.5–4mm (6–10oz) thick, depending on the use. For strength they should ideally be cut out in the direction of the backbone. Sides, backs or butts are the most suitable, but shoulders can be used as long as they are firm. Use a metal straight-edge or rule to mark a line from head to tail. Keep the knife upright and cut through the leather, using the rule as a guide (Fig. 19). Once you have a straight edge, accurately measure the buckle width on the inside. Measure and mark the belt width along the length of the straight edge of the leather. In the same way as before, cut out the belt strip. If you have a plough gauge, strap cutting becomes much easier as it is both quick and accurate. First, set the width of the strap by sliding the fence along the graduated gauge. Holding the knife handle in one hand, push the straight edge of the leather under the roller until it presses against the fence. Push the knife forward, parallel to the edge of the leather and gently pull the emerging belt strip with your other hand (Fig. 20).

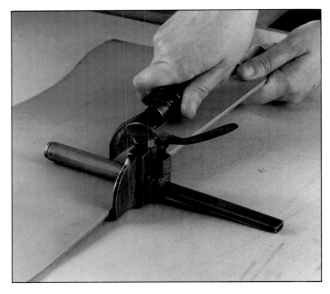

FIG. 20 *Cutting a straight strip of hide using a plough gauge.*

FIG. 19 *Cutting a straight strip of hide using a metal rule and knife.*

6

DYEING AND FINISHING

DYEING

If you cannot obtain pre-dyed leather in the colour you want or if you plan to use decorative techniques, it is possible to dye natural russet yourself. You will achieve better results on full-grain leather than on leather that has had its grain surface 'buffed' to remove imperfections. On leather that has been buffed, the areas where the surface has been broken absorb the dye more quickly and allow it to penetrate more deeply, which gives an uneven effect. To overcome this problem, the currier (the person who dresses and colours tanned leather) adds pigment to the dye,

but if more than a small amount of pigment is used, the resulting colour is flat and uninteresting.

Vegetable tanned leathers darken naturally when they are exposed to light, and no leather, therefore, remains the same colour as it was on the day it was dyed. If it is essential that a stable, long-term colour is achieved, you could experiment with the use of acrylic-based leather paints and dyes. If they are used undiluted, acrylic dyes give a strong surface colour with little or no surface penetration. They can, however, be diluted with water, which makes possible some penetration. Their colours are brighter and more vivid than spirit- and water-based dyes, but if

LEATHER DRESSINGS, POLISHES AND FINISHES

Name	Description and uses	How to apply	Comments
Pliantene	Dressing and polish; can be used on all vegetable tanned leathers; penetrates well; imparts a satin shine; recommended for old leather.	Wear rubber gloves and apply several light coats with a soft cloth; allow to dry, then buff up with a bristle brush; do not use on damp leather.	In cold weather, warm the bottle in hot water to dissolve granules of beeswax but unscrew the top first; work in well-ventilated room; requires long drying time.
Fiebing's 4-Way Care	Dressing and softener; use on any vegetable tanned leather.	Apply liberally to damp or dry leather with a soft cloth; allow to dry then polish.	Good for lubricating brittle or inflexible leathers.
Saddle soap	Cleans workshop-dyed leather; used mainly to clean hide goods — e.g. saddlery and old luggage.	With a piece of damp foam rubber create a lather and apply in circular movements; change the foam regularly; allow to dry then apply polish.	Ideal for removing dye residue from the grain, which is a problem with spirit dyes.
Neutral shoe cream	A soft cream polish that leaves a protective coating and shine.	Apply sparingly with a soft cloth; buff up when dry.	Easy to use and dries clear; wax polishes leave a white 'bloom' on the surface.
Neatlac	Lacquer used to seal and protect natural leathers.	Wear rubber gloves and apply with a cloth, making sure that you cover the whole area; allow to dry thoroughly before flexing.	It can be diluted with Neatlac thinner; a diluted coat can be used to seal softer leathers — e.g., panel hide.

they are used too thickly they mask the grain of the leather and will give a 'plastic' appearance to an article. Acrylic dyes are ideal for painting small decorative patterns or pictures on to the surface of leather.

Before you attempt to dye large areas of leather, you should carry out some tests on small samples using the three types of dye available – that is water-based, spirit-based and acrylic ones. The qualities you should look for are the evenness of colour, the degree of dye penetration, the degree of water-fastness and the stability of the colour when it is exposed to sunlight.

THE DYE BENCH

If possible, position your dye bench near to the sink and next to a window to make sure there is good ventilation. Cover the surface of the bench with plain paper; never use newspaper, because the ink comes off!

CLEANING

Before dyeing, clean the surface of the leather. This is necessary because natural leathers easily pick up grease marks, which inhibit absorption of the dye. Make a mild solution of oxalic acid (5ml/1 teaspoon to 0.5l/1 pint of water) and gently wash the surface of the leather with a piece of soft cloth. Always wear protective gloves and keep the oxalic acid crystals, which are poisonous, in a locked cupboard.

DYEING

Water- and spirit-based dyes

To promote an even absorption and good penetration of dye, use a piece of foam rubber or cotton wool to dampen the leather all over with water. Make a pad from a piece of soft cotton cloth and dip it into the dye. Press the pad on to some scrap leather to remove any excess dye, and then, beginning in one corner, move the pad in small circular movements over the surface of the leather. When necessary, recharge the pad with dye, remove any excess and continue until the whole area has been coated. Turn the leather through 90 degrees and repeat the dyeing process until you have achieved the colour you want.

You will find that it is easier to obtain an even colour if you apply several light coats of diluted dye,

gradually building up the colour, rather than applying a single, heavy coat. Alternatively, you could use an airbrush, which will give good results, but take care! Use it outdoors when there is no wind, and if you do use it indoors, wear a face mask and make sure your workroom is well-ventilated. If you think you will be using an airbrush regularly, you might even want to fit an extractor fan.

Whenever possible, dye the leather before you cut out the pattern pieces because the process of dampening, dyeing and drying causes the leather to shrink slightly.

Acrylic dyes and paints

If you need to cover a large area, acrylic dyes can be used undiluted and applied with a wide brush. Alternatively, they can be diluted with water and applied in several coats using a cloth or an airbrush. Whichever method is used, make sure the leather is dry before you start.

After dyeing, you will have to 'dress' and 'finish' the leather.

FINISHING

Natural leathers will always need 'dressing' or feeding, polishing and finishing if they are used undyed, if they have been dyed in the workshop or if they were bought pre-dyed but appear to be dry and inflexible.

After natural hide has been tanned it is usually 'fat liquored' and oiled by the currier. However, if it is sold in its natural condition, such leather often soon dries out, so it needs careful handling and liberal applications of dressings by you. Although it is possible to dress a large piece – a shoulder, for example – it is more economical to feed just enough leather for a particular project. Take care that you do not get polish or lacquer on to edges that are going to be burnished or on to the flesh side.

BURNISHING

An effective way to seal the surface and impart a good shine to undyed, natural leathers is by 'burnishing', a very simple process. A piece of hard wood, like boxwood, is pushed over the surface of damp leather. The pressure compresses the fibres and seals the grain, leaving a 'glazed' surface.

Making a burnisher

Take a piece of boxwood about 60mm wide by 20mm thick by 100mm high ($2\frac{1}{2} \times \frac{3}{4} \times 4$in). Carefully round off one end so that there are no rough, sharp corners. Rub it with fine sandpaper until the surface is as smooth as silk. Shape the end that you will hold so that it is comfortable and easy to hold. You now have a burnisher.

Lay the leather flat on a smooth, clean bench. Dampen it all over with water and, when the colour begins to lighten, take the burnisher and push it backwards and forwards over the surface (Fig. 21). Make sure that you maintain an even pressure. Notice how the leather darkens as you work and feel how flat the grain has become. Allow the leather to dry completely and then apply Pliantene or neutral shoe cream. Work on enough leather to make your project but do not cut it out until you have finished burnishing or the shapes may distort slightly and cause constructional problems.

FIG. 21 *Surface burnishing natural hide using a boxwood burnisher.*

7

EDGE FINISHING

Neatly finished edges will improve the aesthetic appeal of an item as well as protecting and strengthening it. The choice of construction, and therefore the type of edge finish, will be determined by the design – its size, shape and function – and by the leather – its flexibility and thickness. As a rough guide, articles made from firm leather that is thicker than 1.5mm (4oz) can be 'cut-edged'.

A turned-edge or turned-edge binding is generally used for items made from hide or skins thinner than 1.5mm. A bound edge can be used with almost any leather.

CUT-EDGE FINISHING

Once an item has been cut out, edges that are to be left as single layers – flaps, straps, gusset tops and so on – have to be bevelled and burnished. Edges that are made up of several layers stitched together are finished after stitching.

BEVELLING

Bevelling is the process of removing sharp angles in order to round edges before burnishing. The tools you will need are variously known as edge shaves, edge bevellers or edgers. The most useful sizes are numbers 1, 2 and 3, but to begin with you will probably find that size 2 will be sufficient.

Lay the work on a firm surface, grain side up. Hold the edge beveller in one hand, with the fingers of the other hand holding the leather securely. Push the tool along the edge at an angle of 45 degrees to remove a thin shaving (Fig. 22). This need not be a continuous movement; you can stop to reposition the leather then begin again. Turn the leather over and repeat the process on the flesh side. If the leather is russet or rather dry, you should dampen

the edges slightly before you begin bevelling; this will prevent the tool from dragging and causing a crinkled edge. Leathers less than 1.5mm (4oz) are difficult to bevel, but they can be burnished without bevelling.

When you have stitched two or more layers together, you will need to level them off with a flat knife before bevelling and burnishing them. A paring knife is ideal for this because the flat back of the blade helps to prevent it from digging in.

BURNISHING

Polishing or burnishing the edges of cut-edged work prevents them from becoming ragged or frayed. By sealing the fibres and creating a hard, shiny edge, you will protect the stitching, and the article will be more durable.

Make an edge-burnishing solution by mixing one part paper gum with two parts warm water in a small glass jar. A piece of folded felt held in a clothes peg makes a good applicator. You should dye the edges of coloured leathers a matching colour before burnishing, but take care that you do not have too much dye on the felt or it will bleed into the surface of the leather (Fig. 23).

Apply burnishing solution to about 15cm (6in) of an edge. Take a piece of canvas and rub it quickly backwards and forwards over the area. The friction generates heat, which binds the fibres into a solid, shining edge (Fig. 24). If you try burnishing a longer length, the friction will not be as intense and the result will be disappointing. Edges that are made up of several layers should become fused into one. Make sure that you hold the canvas around the edge when you rub it or the edge will curl over each side. To burnish leather that is thinner than 1.5mm (4oz), lay the work on a flat surface – a litho stone is ideal – and rub first the edge of the grain side, then the flesh side, until a shine is achieved. Saliva is excellent for

FIG. 22 *Removing a thin shaving with an edge beveller.*

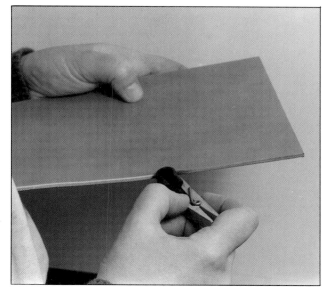

FIG. 23 *Carefully dyeing an edge.*

FIG. 24 *Burnishing an edge.*

burnishing edges, but its use would no doubt be frowned on by your customers!

CREASING

A thin line or crease close to an otherwise plain edge has traditionally been used on a whole range of hand-stitched leatherwork, from saddlery and harnesses to cases and purses. Its function seems to be mainly decorative, but it may strengthen edges by compressing the fibres.

Crease lines are applied after burnishing. Two types of creasing tool are available to the general leather-worker – the single and the screw creaser. A screw creaser has an adjustable guide that sets the line a chosen distance in from the edge, although there is a tendency to lean the tool to one side to prevent the guide from slipping and this creates an uneven impression. A single creaser is more versatile but slightly more difficult to master. Because there is no guide, dividers are used to mark a line for the creaser to follow. Set the dividers to 2–3mm

($1/16$–$1/8$in) and press one point along the edge, leaving a visible line. Heat the creaser over a gas or spirit burner. Test the temperature by placing the heel of the tool on a scrap of the same leather and pushing it forward to reveal a crease line. If the tool is too hot, the line will look scorched and dull; if it is too cool, the creaser will jerk rather than glide smoothly. When it is the correct temperature the creaser should give a dark, polished line. When you are sure that the heat is right, grip the tool firmly and push it forwards (Fig. 25), holding the leather in position with your free hand. For straight lines you can use a ruler as a guide until you feel confident. For curves, tip the tool forwards so that the middle of the iron is in contact with the leather and push it forwards, slowly turning the leather with your other hand. It is important to feel comfortable and in control of the tool or you could let it slip. Take your time and practise on scraps of leather before attempting a project.

FIG. 25 *Creasing a line close to an edge using a hot single creaser.*

FIG. 26 *Establishing the fold line ready for turning.*

FIG. 27 *Using a flat brush to apply PVA adhesive from the glue line towards the edge.*

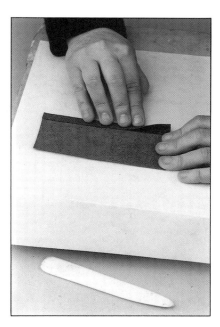

FIG. 28 *Gluing down a turned edge.*

TURNED-EDGE FINISHING

Folding leather back on itself to produce a turned edge is a technique that is particularly useful if you have made a belt, purse, bag, wallet or pocket from leather that is too delicate for a cut-edge finish.

To turn an edge you have to reduce the thickness of the turnover by between a half and two-thirds from just behind the bend. Once the edge has been pared (see Chaper 8), it can be turned and glued. The best way to do this is to lay a metal straight-edge along the fold line and fold the leather into a 90-degree angle with the bone folder (Fig. 26). Apply some PVA adhesive (Fig. 27), and when it is tacky fold the leather down to the glue line (Fig. 28). Press the bone folder along the fold to make sure it is completely glued, then place it under a heavy weight (old telephone directories are ideal) until the glue is dry. Unlined, flat turned edges should not need stitching.

To turn curved edges accurately you should make a turning pattern from thin zinc and use this to fold against instead of the steel rule. Very stiff, thin card will make temporary turning patterns, but they can be used only a few times. An iron-on proprietary stiffener such as Vileden is useful for turning on to, particularly around curves.

BOUND-EDGE FINISHING

An edge can be bound because it needs protecting or to enhance a design. The binding can be a separate strip of leather, glued and stitched around the edge, or it can be a turnover allowance.

SEPARATE BINDING

Calculate the binding width by measuring the depth of layers to be covered then add 12mm ($1/2$in) – that is, 6mm ($1/4$in) to each side – to give the stitching allowance. Pare a hide binding down to a thickness of 0.8–1mm ($1/32$in) (see Chapter 8) but leave skin bindings full thickness. Dye and burnish the edges of the binding (see Chapter 6) but not of the layers to be bound. Glue the binding to one side, marking the position with dividers. When the glue has dried, bend

FIG. 29 *The bound edge of a hide bag, showing a Sam Browne stud closure.*

5 *Detail of a quilted calf bag showing a French binding.*

the binding over and glue it to the other side, using the bone folder and bulldog clips. Mark the stitches 3–4mm ($^1/_8$in) away from the bound edge and stitch (Fig. 29).

FRENCH BINDING

This style of binding should be attempted only when you use delicate leathers such as calf or kid or the results will be too bulky (colour photograph 5). To work out the width of the binding strip, make up a small sample to simulate the layers to be bound. Pare a strip of leather that is wider than you think will be necessary (see Chapter 8). Glue and stitch it 2mm ($^1/_{16}$in) from the edge (Fig. 30). Turn the binding over the edge and glue it to the back. Mark a second row of stitches, 1.5mm ($^3/_{32}$in) below the first row, and stitch. This second row of stitches will catch up the binding that is glued to the back of the edge (Fig. 31).

FIG. 30 *A binding strip stitched into position.*

FIG. 31 *The binding strip wrapped around the edge layers, glued, then stitched in place.*

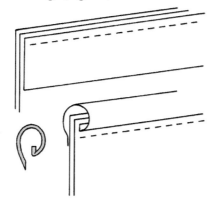

TURNOVER BINDING

You can use turnover bindings when you make bags from hide and skins up to 1.75mm (5oz) thick, which would be too soft for a cut-edge finish. The binding is actually a turnover allowance, wrapped around the raw edges and seams. To calculate the width of the turnover, measure the thickness of the layers to be bound – gussets, linings, pockets and so on – then add a 6mm ($^1/_4$in) stitching allowance.

Pare off enough leather so that it bends with ease; you will need to remove from between one-third and a half of the thickness, but not so much that it becomes weak. Wrap it around the edges and layers to be bound and glue it in position with PVA adhesive. Mark the stitches 3mm ($^1/_8$in) from the turned edge and stitch.

PIPED SEAMS

This method of construction is possible only when you are using flexible leather because the bag has to be made inside out then turned the right way when it has been stitched. Large, soft luggage-style bags can be made in this way provided the leather is no thicker than 1.8mm (5oz). Calf or goat can be used for small bags, but do not use kid because it creases too much. The seams are constructed by folding and gluing a strip of leather around a cord. This piping must be sandwiched between the layers of the seam to be stitched (Fig. 32). A few stitches before the seam ends, the piping should 'disappear', leaving the last few stitches without any piping between the layers. You can then pull the bag carefully through its top opening (colour photograph 6).

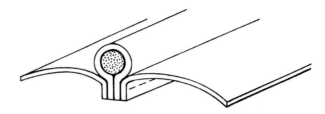

FIG. 32 *A cross-section of a piped seam.*

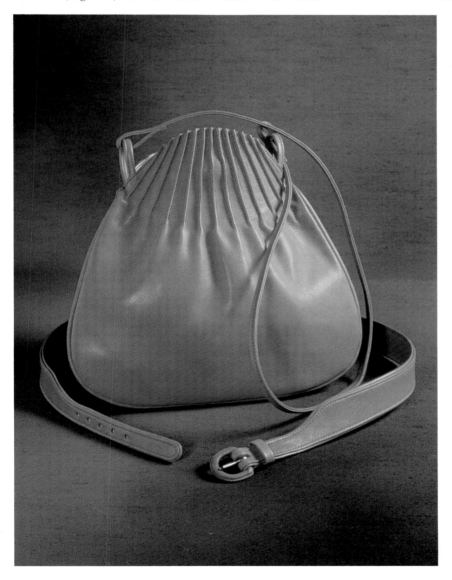

6 *A calf bag made with a piped seam and a matching belt with turned edges.*

8

PARING OR SKIVING, SPLITTING AND CHANNELLING

PARING OR SKIVING

The word paring is commonly used for skins, while skiving is used for hide, but both words describe the same process – that of reducing the thickness of leather for attaching buckles, D-rings and handle fittings, turning edges, lapping together two pieces of leather and bindings.

Paring or skiving is invariably carried out on the flesh side of the leather. Being able to skive accurately will increase your design potential and widen the range of work that you can make. Most paring can be done using a sharp paring knife, but investing in a bench-mounted paring machine would soon repay the outlay. A paring stone, also known as a litho stone, is essential for neat work, but you could manage with a slab of smooth marble. Place the strop beside the stone and use it regularly. It is essential that you keep the knife razor-sharp.

BELTS AND STRAPS

Hide that is thicker than 2.5mm (6oz) that is to be used for belts, handles and straps will need thinning down to help it bend. Reduce the thickness by no more than one-third and begin the skive at least 10mm ($^3/_8$in) from the point at which it must bend around the buckle. Hold the strap firmly and position the paring knife so that the cutting edge is parallel to the end of the strap. Holding the blade at an angle of approximately 30 degrees, push the blade forwards, making a diagonal cut, until it reaches the end (Fig. 33a). Holding the knife at a steeper angle and using the blade, remove any rough fibres from the end of the strap (Fig. 33b). It is a good idea to dampen the

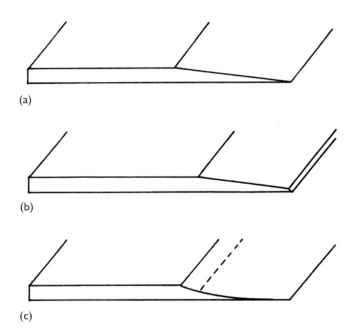

FIG. 33 *A cross-section of pared or skived edges:* (**a**) *for belt and strap ends or for overlapping the joints of bindings;* (**b**) *for a fine edge; and* (**c**) *a turned edge.*

bend and gently fold it back on itself, grain to grain, to avoid the possibility of the surface cracking.

D-ring holders are made from a strip of hide folded in half with the D-ring sandwiched between. The leather enclosing the ring should be left at its full thickness, but the two ends should be reduced by half if the leather is more than 2.5mm (6oz) thick. Skive in the same way as for attaching a buckle.

TURNINGS

A turned edge is a method of edge finishing used on wallets, purses, bags and pocket tops that have been made from skins thinner than 1.5mm (4oz) (see page 37).

First, decide on the width of the turnover; 10mm ($^3/_8$in) should be enough for most work. Use a fine pen to draw a line 10mm ($^3/_8$in) in from the edge on the flesh side of the leather; this is the fold line. Draw another line at 20mm ($^{13}/_{16}$in); this is the glue line.

Method 1

Hold the leather firmly on the litho stone and position the paring knife 2mm ($^1/_{16}$in) behind the fold line at the top left-hand corner. The knife should be at an angle of 45 degrees. Push it down until you can feel it enter the leather, drop your wrist to flatten the angle of the blade and push it forwards to the edge (Fig. 34), so that the depth and angle of the cut resemble that

shown in Fig. 33c. Now move the knife along and repeat the process until the edge has been pared (Fig. 35). Keep the knife sharp by stropping it often. Mistakes happen if the knife is blunt and you exert too much pressure. To remove loose fibres and leave a neat edge, tip the knife to an angle of 45 degrees and place the blade 1mm ($^1/_{32}$in) from the edge and parallel to it. Push the blade from left to right with a slicing action to produce a fine edge (see Fig. 33b).

Method 2

Adjust the gap between the anvil and blade of the paring machine by turning the wing nut at the bottom. Using a scrap of leather, set the paring machine so that the blade removes half the thickness of the leather. Make sure that the anvil is completely parallel. Now slide the right-hand edge of the leather, flesh side up, under the blade (Fig. 36). Using the pen line as a guide, pull the leather from right to left, using

FIG. 34 *Paring an edge on a litho stone using a paring knife.*

FIG. 35 *Finishing paring; the edge is now ready for turning.*

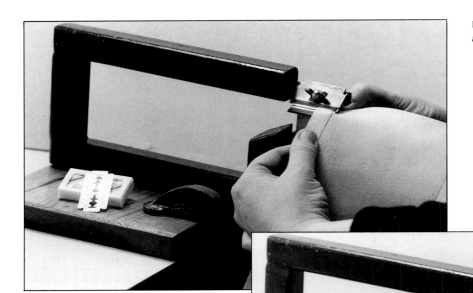

FIG. 36 *Beginning to pare an edge using a paring machine.*

FIG. 37 *Paring the edge along the turnover line.*

the thumb and forefinger of the right hand while holding the leather firmly on the anvil with the fingers of the left hand (Fig. 37). It is essential that you keep the leather under tension over the anvil, or the blade will slice through to the other side. Make a fine edge using the paring knife as previously explained (see page 40).

BINDINGS

Edges can also be bound using a narrow strip of leather (see Chapter 7). This leather binding can be up to 1mm ($^1/_{32}$in) thick for a hide article or only 0.5mm ($^1/_{64}$in) for a calf bag. A paring machine is essential to ensure that the reduction in the thickness of a narrow strip of hide or skin is even. Make sure that the anvil is parallel and, if necessary, remove the thickness in two or three stages.

SPLITTING

Trying to make a bag with gusset leather that is too thick is hard work. If possible, reduce the thickness by splitting it down in a bench-mounted splitting machine. Never remove more than one-third of the thickness or the leather will become stretched and soft.

Use a piece of scrap leather to establish the depth of cut by adjusting the height of the roller. Split a slightly larger piece of leather than you need; it can be cut to size after splitting. Push the pressure release arm back and slide the leather strip, flesh side up, over the roller and under the blade (Fig. 38). Make sure there is enough leather behind the blade to grip with a pair of pliers or your fingers. Keeping the leather level, pull it smoothly through the machine (Fig. 39), dispensing with the pliers once you have

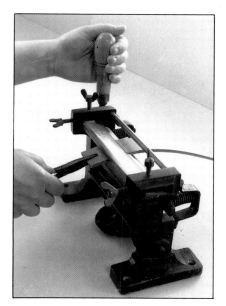

FIG. 38 *A strip of hide, flesh side up, held between the blade and roller of a splitting machine, ready for splitting.*

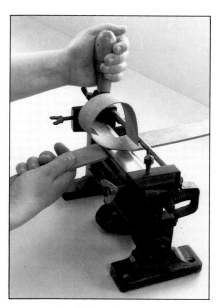

FIG. 39 *Pull the leather smoothly through the splitting machine.*

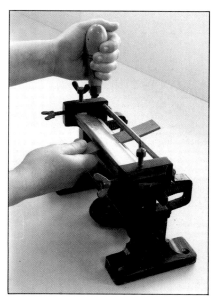

FIG. 40 *Reducing the thickness of a strap or belt end.*

enough leather to hold. The splitting machine can also be used to skive buckle and strap ends as long as the leather is firm (Fig. 40).

CHANNELLING

To shape gussets and right-angled bends in bags, boxes and cases that are made from hide that is thicker than 1.5mm (4oz), you should make a narrow channel along the bend on the flesh side. If you fail to do this the bend is likely to distort and to look bulky. The tool to use is called a race, which has a V- or U-shaped blade. The single race has no guide, so it can be used to race channels across bends using a metal rule as a guide. The compass race is ideal for channelling gussets. It is used by harness makers and saddlers to cut channels for decorative stitching in the grain surface. If the stitches are sunk in this way they will suffer less wear and tear.

Lay the hide on the bench, flesh side up. If it is unwaxed, dampen it with water to soften the fibres. Set the compass width. Holding the leather flat with one hand and the race with the other, draw the race towards you (Fig. 41). Repeat the process until the channel is deep enough to allow the leather to bend without tension. The depth of the channel will depend on the thickness of the leather and its flexibility, but it is unwise to go deeper than half the thickness; one-third would be preferable. Use a metal straight-edge as a guide to cut a channel across a bend. Be careful you do not let it slip!

FIG. 41 *Cutting a channel with a compass race.*

9

GLUING

The most versatile adhesive is leatherworking grade PVA adhesive. It is used to hold gussets and pattern pieces in position ready for stitching, to secure turned edges and to attach linings and reinforcements.

PVA adhesive should be applied with a bristle brush. It readily penetrates the flesh side of leather as long as any wax dressing has been scraped off. Grain surfaces should be abraded to make it easier for the glue to penetrate. It can be thinned down with water, and, because it is water soluble, any traces of PVA adhesive on cut edges will not cause problems when you come to burnish them. Apply PVA adhesive to both surfaces and, when the colour begins to change from white to clear and it feels tacky, bond the surfaces together. Use leather-covered bulldog clips or weights to apply pressure until the adhesive has completely dried. When you are gluing down reinforcements and leather linings, you can apply the adhesive to one surface only as long as you bring the surfaces together while the glue is still white. PVA adhesive remains flexible once it has dried.

Rubber solution is a contact adhesive. It is ideal for holding edges together while you are box stitching and for turning edges of lined belts and bags.

Use a metal or card spreader to apply a thin layer of rubber solution to both surfaces and bond them when it is almost dry. Because the rubber solution does not penetrate well, surfaces can be easily pulled apart. Remember to use it in a well-ventilated room, well away from children, as the fumes are toxic.

METHODS OF APPLICATION

Gussets
Apply a thin layer of PVA adhesive to both surfaces, being careful not to get any on the edges. Bring the surfaces together when the adhesive is tacky and hold them in position with bulldog clips until the adhesive is dry.

Flat work
Wallets, writing cases and pockets need to be held together before they are stitched. Apply lines of PVA adhesive about 5mm ($^1/_4$in) from the edges and use bulldog clips to hold them until the adhesive is dry.

Turned edges
Once an edge has been pared, it is turned and glued, preferably with PVA adhesive. It is a good idea to lay a sheet of paper along the glue line for speed and neatness (Fig. 42). If the edge is to be covered by a lining – if you are making a lined calf belt, for example – you can use rubber solution.

MATERIALS AND TOOLS FOR GLUING

Leatherworking PVA adhesive	Rubber solution	Both
Waxed or greaseproof paper	15mm (5/8in) wide metal spreader	Plain paper
10mm ($^1/_2$in) and 20mm ($^3/_4$in) flat brushes		Bone folder
Old telephone directories		Soft cloth pad
Leather-covered bulldog clips		

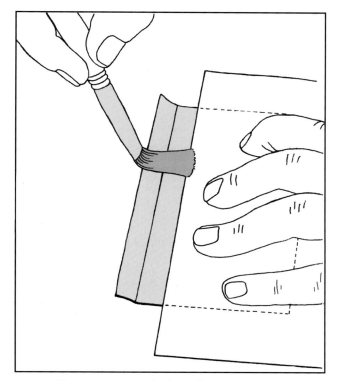

FIG. 42 *Using a paper mask along the glue line.*

Leather linings

Linings that are made of leather are usually glued over the whole area. Cut the lining larger than you need and mark the centres of both the lining and main leather. Apply PVA adhesive to the main leather only. Lay a sheet of greaseproof paper up to the centre marks and glue the lining to the other half, smoothing the lining out from the centre. Ease out the greaseproof paper and glue the other half, using a soft cloth to squeeze out air bubbles and wrinkles (Fig. 43). Press down firmly around the edges. Trim off the excess lining leather with a very sharp knife when the glue is completely dry. Linings attached to curved areas – on bag flaps and belts, for example – should be glued 'on the curve' to stop the bend from puckering (Fig. 44).

Fabric linings

When linings are made of fabric they are usually attached by the edges only and caught in with the stitching of a turned or bound edge. Apply a thin layer of PVA adhesive to the leather and position the fabric while it is still wet. Fabric linings are not suitable for cut-edge work.

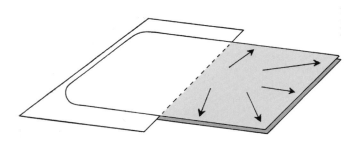

FIG. 43 *Gluing a leather lining to a bag, half at a time.*

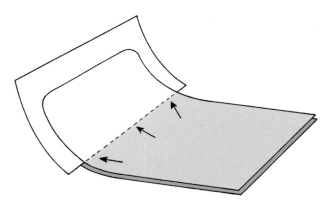

FIG. 44 *Removing the greaseproof paper and gluing the lining to the flap on a curve.*

10

HAND STITCHING

Before you attempt to make any of the projects in this book you must master one, vital technique – hand stitching. If done properly, hand stitching not only looks good but is strong – much stronger, in fact, than machine stitching.

The tools and materials that you will need are an awl, a clam, a pricking iron, dividers, a hide hammer, a knife, a pair of pliers, harness needles, beeswax, linen threads and a bone folder. The length of stitch and the size of the awl, thread and needles will depend on the thickness and density of the leather. The photographs and descriptions explain the techniques of stitching from the point of view of those who are right-handed. If you are left-handed you will need to visualize stitching from left to right, and you will have to hold the awl with your left hand instead of your right.

A 57mm (2¼in) awl blade can be used for most work. Make sure that each facet of the blade is smooth so that it slides almost effortlessly through the leather (see Chapter 2).

SADDLE STITCH

Saddle stitch is the most useful and versatile stitch. It is basically the same stitching technique that is used for box stitching, butt stitching and quilting. Before you attempt to make anything, practise on a double layer of scrap leather, about 3mm (¹⁄₈in) thick, until you feel confident.

1 With the dividers, mark a line 2.5mm (¹⁄₈in) from the edge.

2 Holding the pricking iron firmly with one hand, place it centrally on the line and strike it with the hide hammer to leave a row of slanting slits (Fig. 45). These are intended to be guide marks, so do not attempt to pierce the leather completely. Repeat along the straight lines, positioning the pricking iron two or three marks back into the previous impressions; if you do this it is less likely to slip away from the line. Choose a well-supported area of your workbench or the pricking iron will bounce when struck.

STITCHING RELATIONSHIPS

Leather thickness	Stitches per inch	Thread size	Cord number	Harness needle size	Awl size
1mm or less	12	35	3	6 or 7	45mm (1³⁄₄in)
1.5mm	10	30 or 25	3	5 or 6	51mm (2in)
2.0–2.5mm	8	18	3	5	57mm (2¹⁄₄in)
2.5–4mm	7	18	4	5 or 4	57mm (2¹⁄₄in)
4.0–6mm	7	18	5 and 6	4 or 3	63mm (2¹⁄₂in)

FIG. 45 *Marking stitches with a pricking iron.*

3 To mark around a curve, tip the pricking iron to one side and use only two or three teeth. If you use a pricking wheel proceed very slowly to prevent it wandering off the line.

4 To calculate the length of thread you will need, measure the overall stitching distance and multiply by four. Attach a needle at both ends. If you are using threads thicker than a 3-cord size 18, you will need to taper the ends. Do this by laying the thread end on the bench. Place the blade of a knife on it, about 8cm (3in) from the end. Lean the blade at an angle of 45 degrees towards the end to be tapered and gently pull the thread from under the blade. The thread will unravel and break up. Stop when you have a long fine taper. Repeat at the other end.

5 Beeswax the thread by drawing it repeatedly across the block of wax until it is well coated, especially the ends. Now lock the needles on to the thread (Fig. 46).

6 Position the leather in the clam so that the line to be stitched is along the top. It is important to be comfortable while you stitch. You need to be sitting high enough for your knees to grip the bowed area of the clam, and your feet should rest on a rail or box. If possible, stitch towards you.

7 Take the awl and look at the blade. Turn it until two facets are facing towards you and the

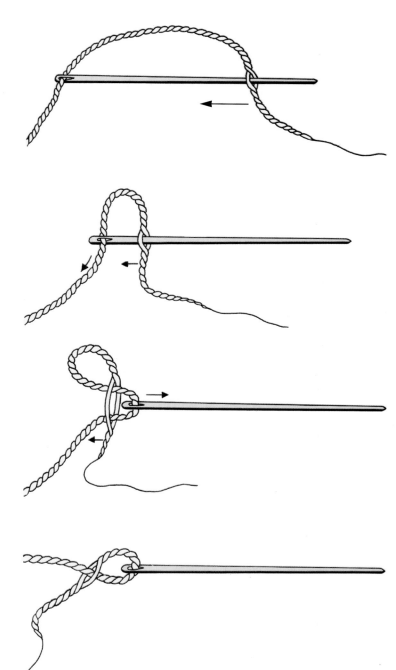

FIG. 46 *Locking a harness needle to the end of a linen thread.*

47

one furthest away is parallel to the top edge of the leather, then pierce the leather through the first mark made by the pricking iron with a quick, thrusting action. Do not wiggle the blade to help it pass through the leather or the hole will be large and round instead of small and diamond-shaped. Keeping hold of the awl, push one needle through the hole and pull the thread until there is an equal amount each side.

8 Holding one needle in the left hand and the other between the index and middle fingers of the right hand, pierce the next hole with the awl (Figs 47 and 48).

9 Allow the awl to rest in the palm of the right hand, supported by the little finger, while you bring the needle forwards and hold it between the thumb and index finger. Push the left needle through the hole (Fig. 49).

10 Place the right needle behind the left to form a cross (Fig. 50), grip the left needle with the thumb and index finger of the right hand and pull the left needle through (Fig. 51).

11 Turn the right hand in an anti-clockwise direction until the tip of the right needle can be slipped into the same hole, positioning it behind the

FIG. 47 *Piercing the second hole with the awl, viewed from the right.*

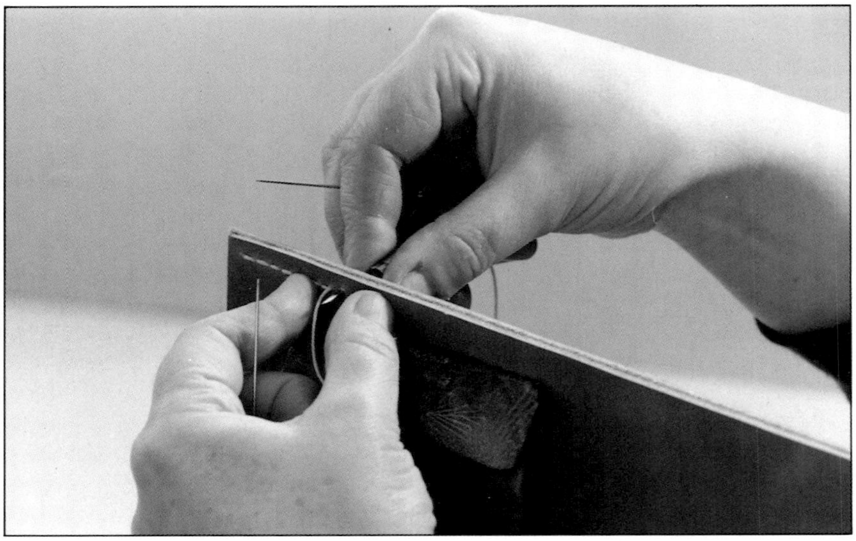

FIG. 48 *The awl emerging on the left, several stitches later.*

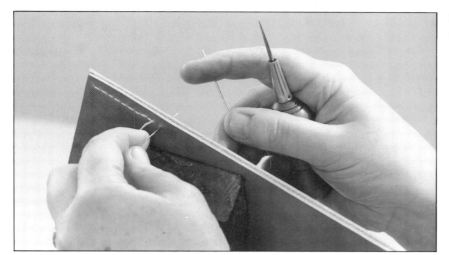

FIG. 49 *The left needle always enters the hole first.*

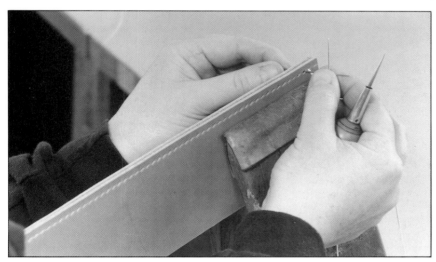

FIG. 50 *The right needle is held behind the left to form a cross.*

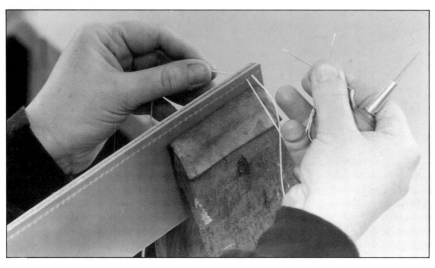

FIG. 51 *The left needle is pulled through.*

thread (Fig. 52). Take care that the needle tip does not pierce the thread (Fig. 53).

12 Cast the thread over the top of the needle (Fig. 54) and pull it through the hole with the thumb and index finger of the left hand (Fig. 55).

13 Pull the stitches in tight, exerting an equal amount of tension with each hand (Fig. 56).

14 Repeat this sequence until you either run out of thread or reach the end of the line of stitching.

Finish off by stitching backwards two or three stitches. Leave both ends at the back of the work and cut them off as close as possible to the stitching.

If you follow this method your stitching will be consistently neat. As long as you do not keep putting down the awl, you will soon develop a rhythm. So persevere until you have the knack.

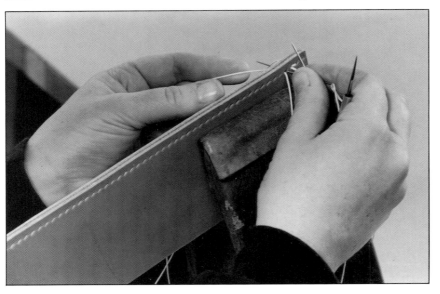

FIG. 52 *The right needle is pushed through.*

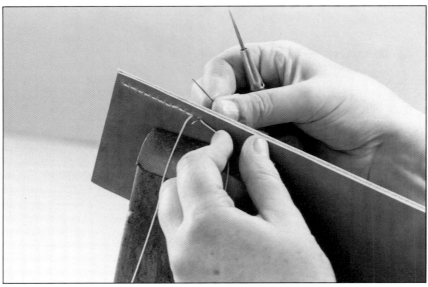

FIG. 53 *Hold the thread out of the way as the right needle emerges.*

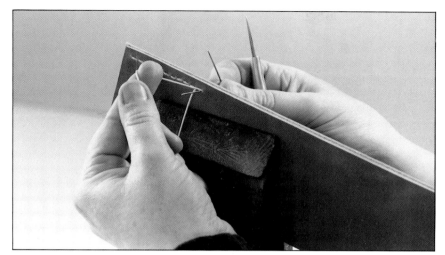

FIG. 54 *Lift the thread over the top of the right needle in the procedure known as casting.*

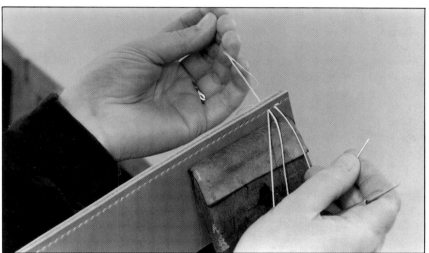

FIG. 55 *Pulling the right needle through.*

FIG. 56 *Evenly 'pulling in' the stitch.*

7 *A pair of hide boxes.*

BOX STITCH

Box stitching is used to make containers, cases, boxes and bags. It is very similar to saddle stitching but the stitches are angled across a corner instead of travelling from one side to the other (Fig. 57). For good results, use firm leather, no less than 2.5mm ($^3/_{32}$in/6oz) thick. Attaché cases should be reinforced with grey board to make them rigid. Bags, purses and containers that are not reinforced should be stitched over a block for support. Blocks can be made either from laminated layers of board or from solid wood.

To understand the technique of box stitching, construct a simple container before attempting anything more adventurous (colour photograph 7).

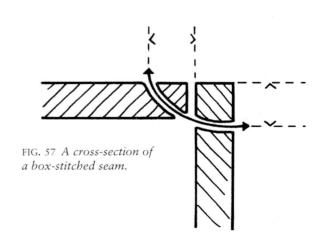

FIG. 57 *A cross-section of a box-stitched seam.*

A SQUARE BOX

1 Cut from 2.5–3mm (6–8oz) hide, a body 10cm wide by 30cm long (4 × 12in) and two sides 97mm (3¹³/₁₆in) square.

Bevel and burnish the two short ends of the body and one edge on each of the sides. Burnish (do not bevel) the two long sides of the body.

2 Across the flesh area of the body, use a race to gouge two shallow channels (see Chapter 8) from side to side, 10cm (4in) from each end.

3 Mark the stitches 3mm (¹/₈in) in from the long edges of the body using a number 7 pricking iron. Mark a corresponding number of stitches around the three edges of the sides.

4 Holding the awl at an angle, pierce the stitch holes in the sides on a block of cork. The awl tip should come out just above the bottom corner (Fig. 58).

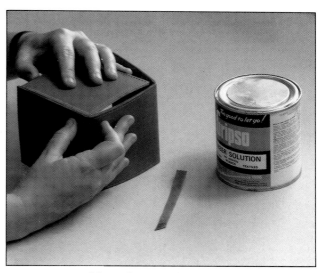

FIG. 59 *Using rubber solution to hold the sides in place before box stitching.*

FIG. 58 *Piercing holes on a cork block ready for box stitching.*

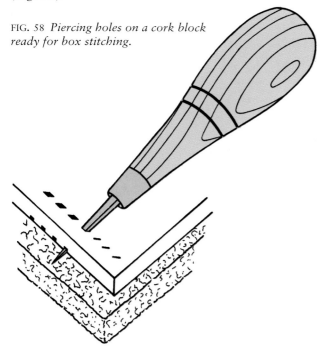

5 Dampen the gouged lines on the flesh and bend the back and front into right angles with a bone folder.

6 Apply rubber solution to the surfaces to be joined and glue the sides in position (Fig. 59).

7 Support the inside of the box with a block and use thick elastic bands to help hold the pieces together while you stitch. Position the box so that the body leather is to the right. Prepare a thread as previously described.

8 Pierce the body leather with the awl, holding it at an angle of 45 degrees, and allow the tip of the blade to locate the corresponding hole in the side. Begin saddle stitching, taking care not to pull the stitches too tightly and without casting the stitches. When you reach the bend, instead of pushing the left needle through the adjacent hole, pierce the hole around the corner on the body and push the left needle through that (Fig. 60). The right needle will

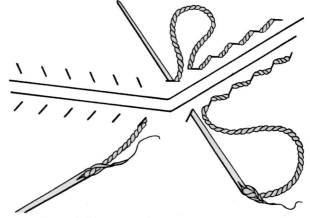

FIG. 60 *Box stitching around a corner.*

complete the stitch by passing from body to side to arrive in the corner hole ready to stitch the base.

To make a lid

1 Cut out the lid body and two lid sides. They need to be wider than the box itself by two thicknesses of leather because the lid has to fit easily over the base and not be too tight.

2 Gouge two channels across the lid; the distance between the channels should be the same as the finished width of the base of the box. Damp them and form them into right angles.

3 Make up the lid in the same way as the box, using the box bottom as the mould on which to stitch.

A circular box can be box stitched in the same way but not before the side seam has been butt stitched together.

BUTT STITCH

Butt stitching, which is known as 'split' or 'round' closing by shoemakers, is a method of joining leather together by passing the stitches through 180 degrees to form a row each side of the join (Fig. 61). Butt stitching used to be used in the construction of many everyday items, including collar boxes, buckets, helmets and sword scabbards, as well as for sewing the back seams of boots and shoes. Like box stitching, it is a useful technique to master because it opens up design possibilities that would otherwise be impossible to explore. As a practical exercise, make a small round box.

FIG. 61 *A cross-section of a butt-stitched seam.*

A ROUND BOX

1 Make a mould from a cylindrical block of wood or a short length of thick cardboard tubing.

2 Cut from 3mm (8oz) hide a body that is long enough to wrap around the block with the edges butted together and a base that has the diameter of the block.

3 Bevel and burnish one long edge of the body, then mark the stitches 3mm ($\frac{1}{8}$in) from the edge. Burnish the other long edge.

4 Mark the stitches with a number 7 pricking iron, 3mm ($\frac{1}{8}$in) in down both sides of the body. Pierce them on the cork block, angling the awl so that the tip comes out at two-thirds of the depth of the leather (Fig. 62).

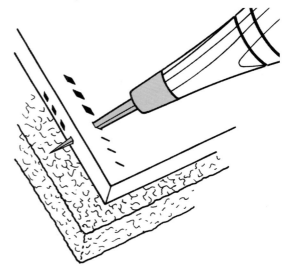

FIG. 62 *Piercing holes in preparation for butt stitching.*

5 If possible, use a number 8 pricking iron to mark the stitches around the base.

6 Wrap the body around the block and hold it together with thick elastic bands.

7 Butt stitch the seam using saddle stitch (Fig. 63). Carefully pull the threads down when you

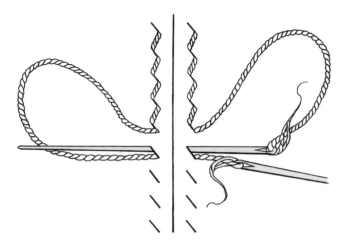

FIG. 63 *Butt stitching.*

tighten the stitches to prevent them from tearing through the grain.

8 Pierce the base for box stitching (Fig. 58). Use rubber solution to glue it in position at the bottom of the body and box stitch the seam together. If the stitches become misaligned, 'lose a stitch' by stitching twice into the same base hole while travelling two holes around the side (see Chapter 18).

Make a lid by using the bottom of the box as the mould.

BACK STITCH

Back stitch is mainly used for repairs and for stitching fabric to leather. Saddlers and bridle makers use it because the long stitch on the back prevents the thread from cutting through fragile leather or fabric as well as looking attractive.

1 Mark the stitches with a pricking iron.

2 Cut a thread that is three times as long as the stitching distance. Taper one end, beeswax it and attach one needle.

3 Position the leather in the clam and pierce the first two marks with the awl.

4 Push the needle and thread through the second hole, from the left, leaving a long end to be caught and woven in with the line of stitching.

5 From the right, push the needle through the preceding hole, pulling it through with your other hand.

6 Still holding the needle in the left hand, pierce the next hole with the awl (Fig. 64).

7 Push the needle through this hole from the left. Pull it to the right, allowing the thumb of the left hand to make a loop (Fig. 65).

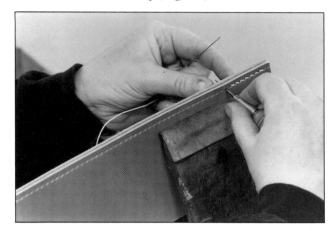

FIG. 64 *Piercing with an awl for back stitching.*

FIG. 65 *The needle is passed through the hole from left to right, the thumb of the left hand at the back forming a loop.*

8 Pass the needle back through the previous hole (Fig. 66), under the loop (Fig. 67). With the right hand, pull the 'back' stitch tight, then tighten the front stitch with the left hand (Fig. 68).

9 Continue stitching to the end. Finish off by stitching back two or three stitches.

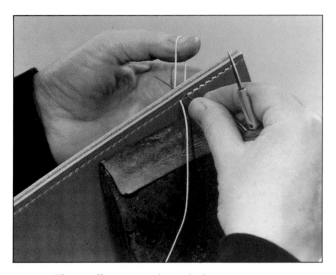

FIG. 66 *The needle passing through the previous hole.*

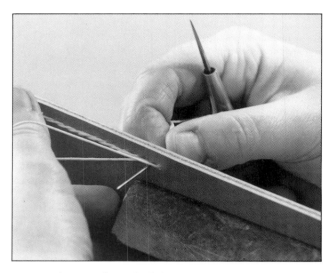

FIG. 67 *The view from the left showing the 'lie' of the stitches.*

FIG. 68 *The right hand pulling the back stitch tight before allowing the left hand to tighten the stitch at the front.*

11

GUSSETS

In Chapter 5, which discussed the basic steps in designing, the need to decide on an appropriate style of gusset at the design stage was emphasized. Preparing simple, practical gussets needs further explanation. It is important that gusset patterns allow for the thickness of leather and the position of the stitching. They determine the height and depth of a bag. If their size is right, their centres correctly marked and their shape well formed, assembly will be straightforward.

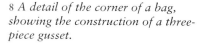

8 A detail of the corner of a bag, showing the construction of a three-piece gusset.

9 A U-shaped gusset, stitched in place and with the edges burnished.

ONE-PIECE CUT-EDGED GUSSET

This style of gusset is used when you are making rounded shaped hide bags. Use hide that is 1.5–2.25mm (4–6oz) thick, if necessary splitting thicker leather down to a workable thickness (see Chapter 8). Determine the length of the gusset by measuring the exact distance around the front of the bag. The width of the gusset will be the proposed finished depth of the bag plus a stitching allowance of 6mm (1/4in) on each side. Once the gusset has been cut out, bevel, burnish and crease the ends (see Chapter 7).

Dampen the flesh area and use a compass race to cut channels 6mm (1/4in) in from each side (see Chapter 8). Now, with the grain facing up, lay a straight-edge 6mm (1/4in) in from the edge and, with a bone folder, bend it into a right angle. When it is dry, the gusset can be glued onto the front and back of the bag and stitched into place. Remember to measure and mark the centre points and to attach D-rings, studs and straps before assembly.

THREE-PIECE CUT-EDGED GUSSET

This style of gusset can be used only when you make rectangular bags or cases – the reason will be self-evident. The two side gussets must be the same measurement as the height of the bag; the base must be the exact width. Using 1.75–2.25mm (5oz) hide, cut out the gusset pieces. Cut out sections 6mm (1/4in) wide from the bottoms of both side pieces and 6mm (1/4in) squares from each corner of the base (Fig. 69). Bevel and burnish the tops and bottoms of

the side pieces. Lay the three pieces, with the grain surface facing down, on the workbench. Dampen the flesh area and, with the compass race set at 6mm (1/4in), cut channels along the edges of each piece. Cut channels across the ends of the base. Turn the gussets over and, while the leather is still damp, bend them into right angles using a metal straight-edge and a bone folder. Cut 1mm (1/32in) slits in the corners of the base where the gouge lines meet (Fig. 70). Bend the base ends into right angles towards the flesh side. When the leather is dry, mark the stitches along the bottom of the sides with a number 7 prick-

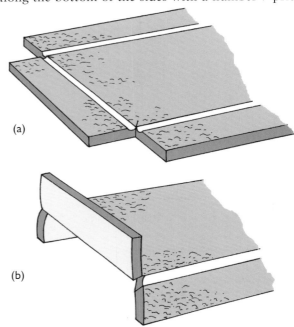

(a)

(b)

FIG. 70 **(a)** *channels cut in the flesh side around the base gusset; and* **(b)** *the shape of the base gusset after the sides and ends have been formed.*

FIG. 69 *Interlocking sections of a three-piece gusset.*

6mm(1/4in)

6mm(1/4in)

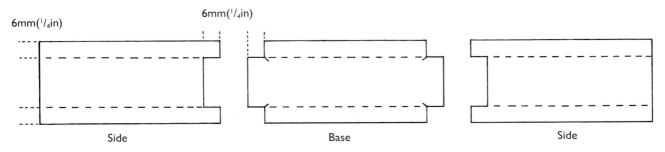

Side   Base   Side

ing iron and pierce them with an awl on a cork block. Glue the sides to the base (Fig. 71) and saddle stitch them together.

The perfect three-piece gusset will form a neat right angle and reveal no gaps when glued and stitched to the bag body (colour photograph 8, page 57).

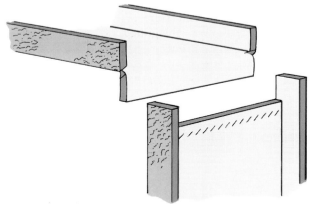

FIG. 71 *The gusset side and base ready for gluing and stitching.*

U-SHAPED CUT-EDGED GUSSET

This type of gusset is used for making bags of which the front, base, back and flap are cut from one piece of leather. They are U-shaped so that they fit into each side. Cut them from 1.5–2mm (4–5oz) hide. Bevel, burnish and crease the tops before shaping. Dampen the flesh side and, using a compass race, cut a channel 10mm (1/2in) in from the edges of the U shape. While the leather is still damp, form this lip into right angles and leave it to dry completely before you assemble the bag. To ensure consistently good results, it is a good idea to make a simple two-piece mould.

From 10mm (3/8in) plywood, cut out a U shape the size of the finished gusset and screw the piece of wood from which you have cut the U shape to a flat plywood base. Reduce the size of the U-shaped piece by 2mm (1/16in) all around to allow for the thickness of the leather.

To shape a gusset, dampen the leather again after the channels have been cut and begin to bend the sides up. Place the gusset, grain side up, on the base of the mould and push the wooden U shape down onto it, forcing the leather into shape (Fig. 72). Hold the mould together with a G-cramp until the gusset is dry. It is now ready to be glued and stitched into position (colour photograph 9, page 57).

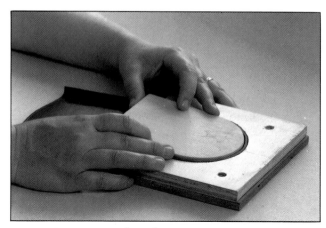

FIG. 72 *Forming a U-shaped gusset in a mould.*

U-SHAPED BOUND-EDGED GUSSET

This kind of gusset is used when you make bags with a turned-edge binding from soft hide or firm skins up to 1.5mm (approximately 1/16in/4oz) thick. The edges of the gussets are bound by a turning allowance on the bag body. Cut out the gussets, leaving a turned-edge allowance of 10mm (3/8in) at the tops. If the bag is lined, glue in the gusset linings before you turn over the pared gusset tops and stitch them down. If the gussets are unlined, the tops can be turned but need not be stitched. Because the leather is thinner and more flexible than the hide used for cut-edged work, you do not need to use a race to make a channel at the turn line. But the gusset will need to be shaped, and you can use either a mould or a piece of stiff card that is 10mm (3/8in) smaller than the gusset to form a simple turning pattern. Place the mould or card on the grain side, leaving a 10mm (3/8in) gap all round. With the tip of the bone folder, mark a line around the turning pattern, then shape the 10mm (3/8in) allowance into a right angle. If the leather immediately springs back, dampen the flesh side and try again. When it is dry, glue the gussets in position by gluing the centres and tops together first. If you seem to have too much leather around the curves, form it into small pleats with the tip of the bone folder and press them down smoothly. Glue the turning allowance around the edges and stitch the gussets in place. The large shoulder bag in Chapter 18 uses this style of gusset.

12

POCKETS

Complicated, zipped, multi-pocketed bags can be successfully made only from lightweight, chrome tanned leathers, not from the vegetable tanned leathers used throughout this book. Vegetable tanning makes strong leather but, because it is heavier than chrome tanned leather, it is important to keep pocket designs simple and to a minimum or your bag will become impracticable. A well-made hide bag will outlast even the best zips, so use them only if you must.

Before you decide on the size and shape of a pocket, you must think about its likely use. A cheque book, passport, driving licence, photographs or cheque cards will all live happily in a flat pocket. Bulkier items – wallets, purses, keys, make-up and so on – need a gusseted pocket. Large items, such as books, a diary, personal organizer and folders, will easily survive in the main area of a bag.

Pockets made from leather that is thinner than 0.6mm (2oz) should have edges turned across single layers. Pigskin and calf up to 1.0mm (3oz) thick make excellent pockets. The pockets inside lined bags should be stitched to the lining before it is glued to the body leather.

FLAT POCKETS

The easiest pockets to make are flat pockets. They can be used inside cut- or turned-edged work or on the outside of cut-edged bags and cases. The top of an internal pocket should be at least 10mm ($^3/_8$in) wider than the bottom to improve accessibility (Fig. 73). Prepare the pocket by turning the top edge (if necessary) and paring the other three sides 10mm ($^3/_8$in) in from the edges, reducing the thickness by a half. Crease a line close to the top edge. Glue it into position inside the bag. If the bag is unlined, stitch the pocket in with a main seam. The edge of the

pocket will either merge into the burnished edge or be covered by a binding. In lined bags, the pocket is stitched to the lining.

GUSSETED POCKETS

THREE-PIECE GUSSETS

These are used to make rectangular pockets. They are prepared and attached in the same way as bag gussets (see page 59) except that the shaping can be done with a bone folder, instead of a race, because the leather is much thinner. The pocket front should be stitched to the gusset and the edges burnished before the pocket is glued and stitched to the flesh side of the bag body. These stitches must be carefully marked on the outside of the bag.

PLEATED GUSSETS

This is a simple pocket, made by adding folding allowances to the sides of an otherwise flat pocket to make pleated side gussets (Fig. 74). Remember to reduce the thickness of the leather at the base of the pleated area by half before stitching the pocket sides to the bag. Glue the pleats together at the base then stitch the pocket bottom in position.

HANGING POCKETS

Hanging pockets are generally used inside large bags or in bags that are an unusual shape. The pocket is suspended from a row of stitching at the back of the bag. They can be made flat or gusseted (Fig. 75).

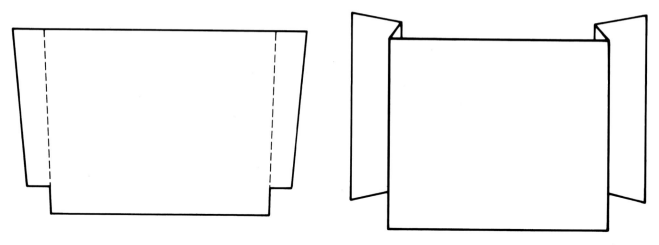

FIG. 73 *A flat pocket.*

FIG. 74 *A side-pleated pocket.*

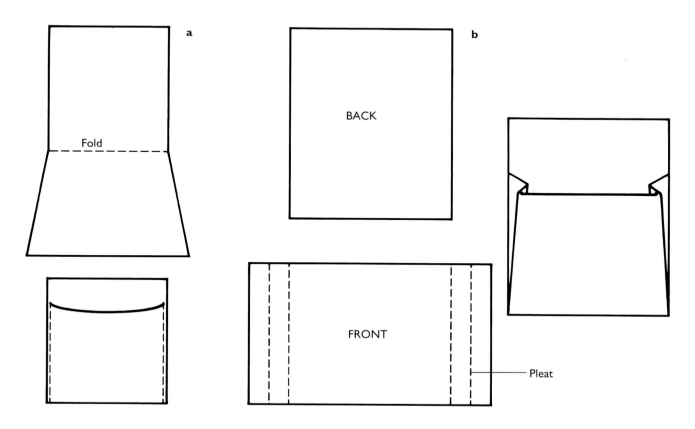

FIG. 75 *Hanging pockets:* (**a**) *a flat pocket;* (**b**) *a pocket with side pleats.*

13

ATTACHING LOCKS, BUCKLES AND STUDS

Some of the most useful metal fittings were described in Chapter 4. The function of these fittings is to provide secure means of closing leather goods or of closing and attaching straps and handles. You should always decide on the style of fittings you want to use at the design stage, rather than leaving your options open until the item is half-made. Whenever possible, use good quality fittings and fit them with the correct tools. (Names and addresses of suppliers are on page 117.)

LOCKS

Because of the wide variety of case locks that is available, it is not possible to explain how to fix each one; in most cases it will be obvious what you should do. Many of the locks manufactured in Europe are made with pointed prongs projecting from the back of the hasp and body. You fix this kind of lock in place by cutting slits in the leather, pushing the prongs through and bending them on to a backing plate. A leather washer, glued over the back of the lock, prevents the metal from damaging fingers and bag contents.

Locks made in the UK are held in place with solid and split rivets (Fig. 76). The top of a lock, the hasp, is attached to the flap by marking and punching the rivet holes with the smallest size punch, and then positioning the hasp and backing plate so that the holes correspond. If the holes in the hasp or body are too small, use a pin-hole needle (rat's-tail file) to open them enough for the rivet to fit snugly. Push the solid rivets through the holes with the domed end on the hasp front. Any surplus length should be cut off with a pair of metal snips, but remember to allow about

FIG. 76 *A close-up of a folio lock held in place with brass rivets.*

1mm ($\frac{1}{32}$in) for doming over on to the backing plate on the inside. Place the rivet head in the hasp on a lead block and protect the hasp with a layer of tissue. Using a metal hammer, place a doming punch over the rivet tip and gently tap it, slowly rotating it as you do so, to round off the rivet top and fix it to the backing plate (Fig. 77). The steps involved in fixing a lock bottom are illustrated in Fig. 78.

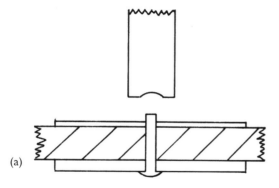

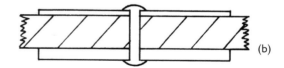

FIG. 77 *A cross-section showing a solid brass rivet going through the lock hasp, leather and backing plate; (a) before doming; and (b) after doming.*

FIG. 78 *Attaching a lock.*

1 Determine where the lock is to be positioned and put the backing plate in place. Use a scratch awl to mark the hole to be cut out and the rivet holes. Find the centre and, with your dividers, mark a stitch line 2mm ($^1/_{16}$in) larger than the backing plate. Pierce the centre hole through to the back.

2 On the back – this is the flesh side if your bag is unlined – use the centre hole to mark the position of the leather washer, making it 2mm ($^1/_{16}$in) larger than the diameter of the stitch line. Scratch the area in the circle with sandpaper to help the washer stick.

3 Cut out the lock position. Punch the rivet holes and mark the stitching.

4 Back view.

5 Position the lock and fix it in place with split rivets.

6 Back view with backing plate in place.

7 and **8** The washer glued and stitched in place.

BUCKLES

Buckles are available in a variety of sizes and shapes (Fig. 79). Bear the type of leather and its proposed use in mind when you choose a buckle. Solid ones are heavier than plated ones, so whole buckles are generally too bulky to use on most leather goods, although, if they are not too big, they can be useful for hide belts. It is better to use half-buckles (also known as single buckles) to fasten bag flaps because they are lighter.

To use a buckle to close a bag, make a buckle holder in a similar way to a D-ring holder (see Chapter 8). If the leather is thicker than 2.5mm (6oz) it will need skiving. You should stitch the buckle holder to the bag front before you make up the bag. A short strap, the billet, must be prepared and stitched to the flap (Fig. 80). The large shoulder bag in Chapter 18 uses this style of bag closure.

Making a hide belt is described in Chapter 16, and because strap buckles are attached in exactly the same way, if you know how to make a belt you will be able to make other types of strap.

A feature of some old harness and leather goods is the use they make of leather-covered buckles. It is possible and not too difficult for you to cover simple curved single buckles and D-rings with leather too. The leather can be hide or skin, but it should be no thicker than 0.6mm (2oz), so it might be necessary to pare the leather down using the paring machine. Shapes and sizes of buckle vary so much that it is impossible to give precise cutting dimensions (colour photograph 10).

FIG. 80 *A billet stitched to a flap.*

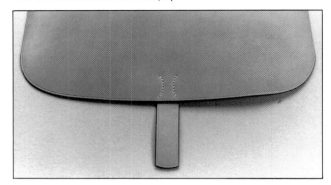

FIG. 79 *Some examples of belts and buckles.*

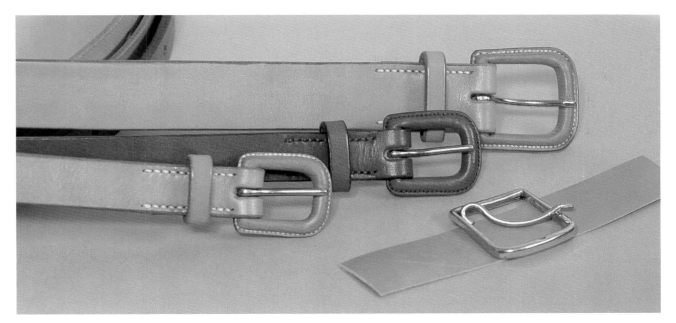

10 *Leather-covered buckles.*

MAKING A LEATHER-COVERED BUCKLE

1 Begin by removing the buckle tongue in a vice.

2 Cut a strip of leather, longer than you think necessary and wide enough to wrap around the buckle leaving a 5mm ($^3/_{16}$in) lip each side.

3 Cut a V shape from one end.

4 Thoroughly wet the leather and fold it in half lengthways. Mould it around the inside of the buckle, beginning at the point where the tongue should be attached. Stretch and pull the leather slowly into shape, using leather-covered bulldog clips to keep it in place. You will probably need to go back and forth, pulling and readjusting the leather until the shape is right. Trim off any excess length, cut a V in this end and hold it place (Fig. 81).

5 When the leather is dry, remove the clips and apply PVA adhesive to the inside of the lip. Hold the edges together until the glue has set.

6 Using a pricking wheel or iron that will give between 12 and 18 stitches to the inch – the

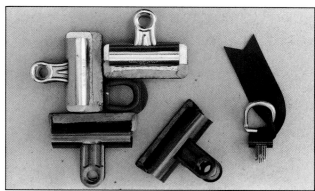

FIG. 81 *Moulding dampened leather around a buckle with the aid of leather-covered bulldog clips.*

number will depend on the size of the buckle and your eyes – mark the stitches close to the buckle shape.

7 Gently hold the buckle in the clam, and, using a small awl, stitch the leather around the buckle using a size 30 or 35 linen thread.

8 Trim away the excess leather to within 2mm ($^1/_{16}$in) of the stitching and burnish the edge.

9 Carefully re-attach the tongue.

STUDS

A variety of studs in different styles, sizes and finishes is available, and they all require different tools to fix them in place.

PRESS-STUDS

Press-stud is the name given to a type of lightweight stud used on small leather goods. These studs come in four pieces, which are fixed in pairs by using special hand tools for each size and type. The top has a domed front, which is fixed to the head through a small hole in the leather. Bases are attached in much the same way. Be sure to use the correct setting tools and to keep them with their corresponding studs to avoid any mix ups. Durable dots are stronger and easier to fix than standard press-studs, so use these if you can (Fig. 82).

FIG. 82 *A cross-section showing how to fix a durable dot type press-stud: (a) the head; and (b) the base.*

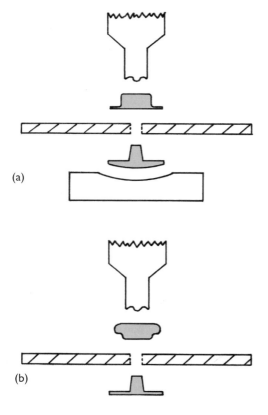

(a)

(b)

SCREW STUDS

Screw studs offer a simple method of securing bag flaps and attaching straps (see the box bag project in Chapter 18). They are the easiest studs to use as no special tools are required to fix them. They come in two parts: the base is screwed into the head through a hole that is punched in the leather (Fig. 83). If possible, use a vice to hold the head while you tighten the screw, but cover the jaws of the vice to avoid damaging the stud.

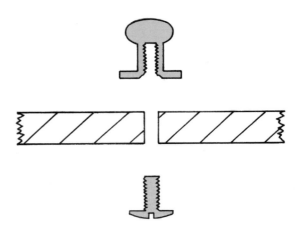

FIG. 83 *A cross-section showing how a screw stud is attached.*

A practical and attractive way of closing a bag can be made using a screw stud and a D-ring. The stud is fixed to a short length of strap that is wide enough to pass through the curve of the D-ring. The strap is then stitched to the front of the case or bag. A strip of leather, a D-ring holder, is stitched to the flap, allowing the screw stud strap to pass through the D-ring, fold back on itself and fix over the head of the stud (Fig. 84).

FIG. 84 *Using a screw stud and D-ring to close a bag.*

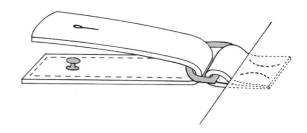

SAM BROWNE STUDS

These solid brass studs are larger than screw studs. They are fixed in place by a metal washer on the back, and the shank is hammered flat on to it. Stitch a leather washer over the back (see Fig. 29).

MAGNETIC STUDS

Magnetic studs provide an excellent means of invisible closure. They are fixed to a leather lining by pushing the short metal prongs through small slits in the leather and bending them flat over a metal washer (see the wallet and passport holder project in Chapter 17).

Sometimes holes need to be made too far from the edges of the leather for the revolving punch to reach. If you do not have any single punches, you can make these holes by turning the revolving punch wheel until the required size punch is at the top. Place a scrap of thick hide on the anvil, squeeze the plier handles together and hold it upside-down. Make the hole by hitting the punch with a hide or wooden mallet (Fig. 85).

FIG. 85 *Making a hole with a revolving punch.*

14

STRAPS AND HANDLES

Most bags and cases need a carrying strap or a handle. The style, the length, width and method of attachment should all be thought about and decided on at the design stage. A bag will only be as strong as its weakest point, and this often turns out to be the strap or handle. Always cut them from leather with a tight fibre structure, which invariably means cutting from the middle area of the butt or back. Cut in the direction of the spine, never across the hide or skin, unless you have no choice.

SHOULDER STRAPS

HIDE

Flat straps should be made from 2.5–3.5mm (6–9oz) hide, cut from the back or butt, because they must be capable of taking a lot of strain and wear. Hide shoulder will stretch, so only use it if it is of an even thickness and really firm. The width of straps can vary between 15 and 25mm ($^5/_8$–1in) depending on the size of the bag. If you make them too wide, 35mm ($1^3/_8$in) or more, they will slip from the shoulder.

The simplest and quickest style of strap is made from a single strip of firm hide, which has been bevelled, burnished and creased, and is attached to the bag without any form of adjustment – see the strap used on the box bag in Chapter 18, for example. The obvious disadvantage of this strap is that the length is fixed. The simplest way to make the strap adjustable is to attach a buckle. To calculate the finished length of an adjustable strap, drape a soft tape-measure over one shoulder and either allow it to hang or hold it diagonally across your body. Decide where the bag should 'sit' and measure this length. Add another 250–350mm (10–14in), which will give an adjustment allowance of 10–20cm (4–8in) – that is, about 50mm (2in) for wrapping around the buckle and two

50mm (2in) allowances for attaching to D-rings or for stitching the strap directly to the bag. Cut the strap to the width of the buckle and the D-rings using a metal rule or a plough gauge (see Chapter 5). The strap itself needs to be cut into two pieces. The billet strip should be at least three times longer than the buckle strip so that the buckle does not rest on and rub the shoulder. Skive the end that is to wrap

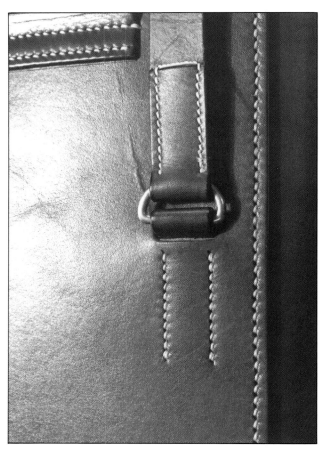

FIG. 86 *Using a D-ring stitched through a slot in a bag to attach a shoulder strap.*

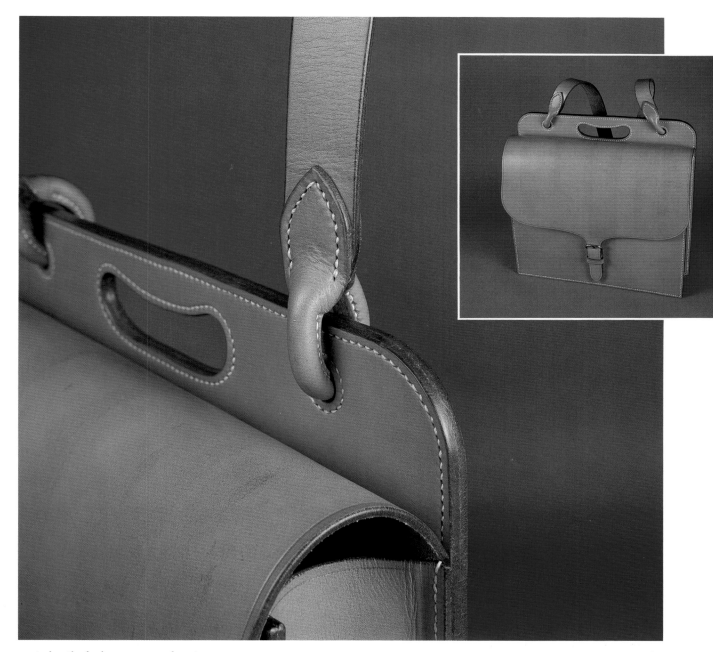

11 *A detail of a bag strap made using a rounding.*

around the buckle and the ends that will attach to the D-rings (see Chapter 8). Cut a strap loop, which is also known as a keeper, that is 10mm ($^3/_8$in) wide. Edge bevel, burnish and crease the strap and the loop. Attach the buckle in exactly the same way as a belt buckle. If the strap is to be stitched directly on to the bag, skive a steep bevel 10mm ($^3/_8$in) from the strap ends. Glue the strap ends in position, then stitch them to the bag before the bag is assembled. If D-rings are used, you will have to make a pair of holders. These are short lengths of hide, folded around the D-ring, and then stitched to the bag (Fig. 86). The leather enclosing the D-ring should be left at full thickness, but the ends are skived.

SKIN

Lightweight bags need straps that look delicate but that are, in fact, strong. One way to achieve this is by folding a strip of leather into several layers (Fig. 87).

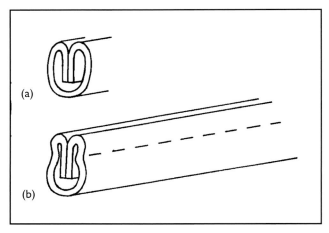

FIG. 87 *A folded calf strap:* (**a**) *before stitching; and* (**b**) *after stitching.*

To make a calf strap with a finished width of 8mm ($^5/_{16}$in) cut a strip of leather 28mm (about $1^1/_8$in) wide. Mark a line down the centre on the flesh side. Fold each side to within 1mm ($^1/_{32}$in) of this central line and glue them in position. Fold and glue the strap in half. Mark the stitches with a number 10 pricking iron, 3mm ($^1/_8$in) from the double edge, and pierce them on a block of cork. Now stitch the strap together in the clamp. To attach the strap to the bag, stitch it to the gusset through a slot or catch it in with a main seam.

Another way to make a strap for a lightweight bag is to glue and stitch two narrow strips of skin together. For calf or pig that is thicker than 0.75mm (2oz) the strap need not be reinforced, and it could have a cut-edged finish – that is, dyed and edge-burnished after stitching. However, if the leather is a delicate kid or calf, a reinforcement layer, such as a proprietary stiffener or a strip of thin leather, should be added. The top layer would then need a turning allowance so that its edges could be turned onto the reinforcement before the bottom layer (the lining) is glued and stitched into place.

HANDLES

The most important requirements of a handle are comfort and strength. If a handle feels uncomfortable because it is too wide for the hand or too small to grip, the bag or case will be a nuisance rather than a joy to use. As an experiment, hold strips of leather of different widths and thickness in your hand. Feel the differences between them. Do the same with other materials – rope and wooden dowel, for example. Your hand is likely to tell you that a good shape to hold is one that is rounded and slightly flexible and that responds to the shape of your hand.

ROUND HANDLES

A round handle or 'rounding' is formed by stitching the leather around a cord, rope or dowel core. Because core diameters vary, it is not possible to give cutting measurements. There are two styles of round handle.

Butt stitched

Butt stitching is mainly used to cover rigid dowel handles with leather, but it can also be used to cover rope or cord (Fig. 88). The leather should be no more than 1.75mm (5oz) thick, so it may need to be skived or split (see Chapter 8). It should be cut out in the direction of the back bone. Establish the width of the leather strip by wrapping a scrap around the core; make sure that the edges butt neatly together. Burnish the ends if they are to be flush with the dowel ends or shape them if they are to be stitched to the bag. Beginning in exactly the same place both sides, mark the stitches down each edge of the strip, 3mm ($^1/_8$in) in. Pierce the holes on a cork block as for butt stitching (see Chapter 10). Draw a line along the length of the dowel or cord and, using rubber solution, glue the leather in place, using the line to keep the join level. Carefully butt stitch together.

Saddle stitched

Saddle-stitched handles are made around a flexible rope or cord core (Fig. 89). The leather can be up to 2.5mm (6oz) thick. Work out the width you will need by wrapping a small scrap of leather around the core and adding a stitching allowance of 7mm (about $^1/_4$in) – i.e. 3.5mm ($^1/_8$in) each side. Prepare the ends of the handle ready for attaching to the bag before you make the rounding. Do this by cutting the ends

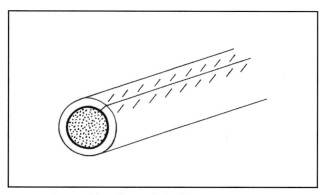

FIG. 88 *A round handle made by butt stitching leather around a rope or a wooden core.*

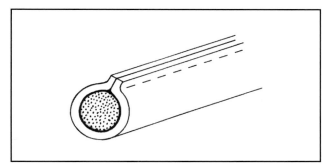

FIG. 89 *A round handle made by saddle stitching leather around a rope or cord core.*

to shape, finish the edges and mark the stitching. To make the rounding, carefully mark the points where the stitching will begin and end along one edge of the grain side and mark the stitching. Along the opposite edge, mark the stitching on the flesh side and pierce these holes on the cork. Dampen the leather to help it bend around the core and, holding the rounding in a clamp, saddle stitch the edges together. The pre-pierced holes on the flesh side of the leather gives the tip of your awl somewhere to aim for and should prevent the stitching from becoming twisted. Take extra care when you do this that the leather is damp but not wet or the stitches will cut through the leather surface when you pull them tight. Only experience and observation can guide you in this. Trim the edge, and bevel and burnish it, ready for attaching to your bag. A miniature version of this handle can be made to attach a shoulder strap (colour photograph 11, page 69).

FLAT HANDLES

Several different styles of 'flat' handle are used on brief cases, attaché cases and boxes. A simple handle that can be used on all these items can be made by folding a strip of leather into three layers, placing a D-ring at each end and stitching them together (Fig. 90). This style of handle is used for the small brief-case project in Chapter 17.

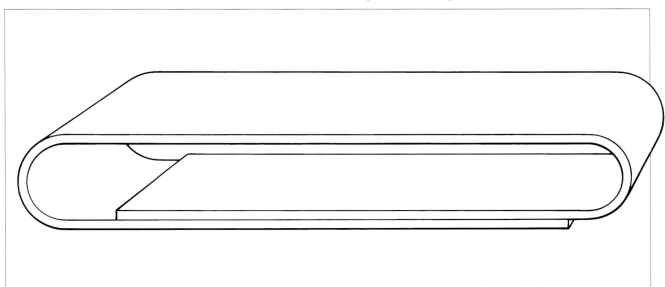

FIG. 90 *A flat handle made by folding a piece of leather into three layers.*

15

MOULDING AND SURFACE DECORATION

MOULDING

An important and potentially creative characteristic of vegetable tanned leather is its ability to maintain a moulded shape. Techniques for achieving this have been exploited for hundreds of years throughout the world, and objects as diverse as boxes, shields, pistol holders, drinking vessels, wall hangings, helmets and sculptures have all been produced using one of the following methods.

When vegetable tanned leather is immersed in water the fibres become soft and pliable. In this state, the surface will readily accept decorative impressions,

12 A moulded hide purse attached to a hide belt lined with pigskin.

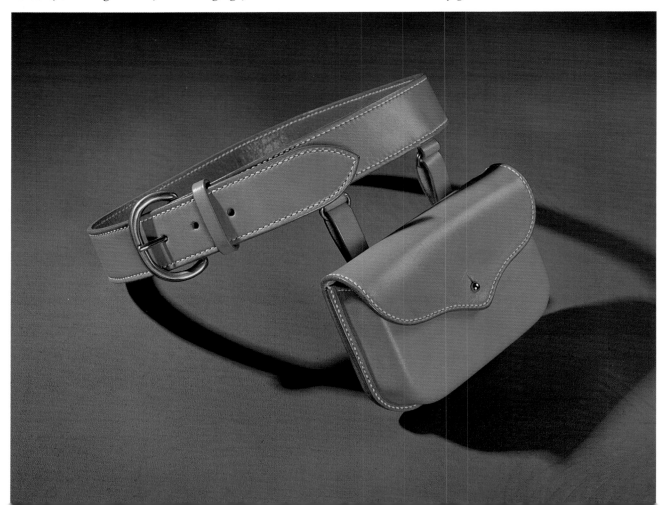

FIG. 91 *Three types of mould:*
(**a**) *three-piece;* (**b**) *two-piece; and*
(**c**) *a one-piece 'last'.*

which are retained even when the leather has dried. While it is saturated, the leather can be formed into three-dimensional shapes between moulds or it can be stretched and easily manipulated by hand. Warm water and a gentle heat can be used to speed up the process.

FREE-FORM MOULDING

As an exercise in free-form moulding, make a simple mask from inexpensive russet belly as described in Chapter 16. Alternatively, soak some small scraps and manipulate them between your fingers. Cut, curl and twist thin strands of leather into spirals and knots or make them into leaves and simple flowers. When you have played enough, place your experi-

ments on a flat piece of wood and heat them gently in an oven, set to its lowest temperature, for a minute or two. This will set the shapes and harden them slightly, but make sure that the leather does not become too hot or your experiments will disintegrate into a contorted mess!

WOODEN MOULDS

To achieve controlled, repeatable moulded shapes, you will have to use a mould or former (Fig. 91).

Three-piece moulds
The simplest way to make a flat bag or purse with no gusset but with some internal space is to force a mould inside it once it has been stitched. To make

this possible, the mould must be cut into three pieces. Make a purse using a three-piece mould as an exercise in this method of moulding (Fig. 92).

1 Make a mould from 10mm (³/₈in) plywood and apply a wax finish (this will make it easier to remove).

2 Cut out the two purse pieces, then position and attach a durable dot (see Chapter 13).

3 Stitch the purse together (see Chapter 10).

4 Completely submerge the purse in warm water.

5 Push the two side sections of the mould inside the purse, keeping them level.

6 Force the central wedge between them until all three are level with the purse front.

7 Allow the purse to dry naturally, then remove the mould pieces with pliers.

8 Bevel and burnish the edges (see Chapter 7).

A three-piece mould can be successfully used only for shallow forming. To create any depth or definition, the leather must be shaped over a mould and held in position until dry.

Two-piece moulds

One method of shaping wet leather into a defined shape is to sandwich it between a two-piece mould and hold it there until the leather has dried naturally. This method was probably used to shape leather shields, and it was certainly used to make series of leather wall hangings. A step-by-step explanation of this method can be found in Chapter 18, where the making of a moulded shoulder bag is described.

One-piece moulds

The technique for shaping a shoe upper, known as lasting, is made possible by stretching the leather over a wooden former or last. This method of shaping leather into a three-dimensional form can be adapted and used to wet-mould leather into quite extreme

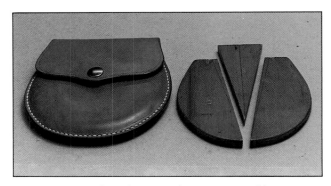

FIG. 92 *A purse shaped using a three-piece mould.*

FIG. 93 *A mask formed by stretching wet leather over a carved wooden mould or last, holding it down with tacks until it is dry, then cutting it from the mould.*

shapes (Fig. 93). Once a mould has been carved to shape, an oversized piece of wet leather is stretched, then nailed over it. You will be surprised how much the leather will stretch, and the nails have to be constantly repositioned until you achieve the shape you want. Once the leather has dried naturally, it can be cut from the mould and made up (colour photograph 13, page 76).

SURFACE DECORATION

A well-known and widely exploited quality of vegetable tanned leathers is the readiness with which they accept surface impressions when they are damp. This is known as tooling or stamping, and it is very simple to do. To begin you will need some decorative stamps and a hide hammer. For incising lines, which is often wrongly called 'carving', you will need a swivel knife (Fig. 94).

Take a piece of foam rubber and use it to dampen a piece of hide with water. The leather should be no thinner than 1.5mm (4oz). Begin tooling when the leather is damp, not wet. If it is too dry the impression will spring back; if it is too wet, the tool will go through the surface rather than leaving an impression. Keep a scrap of leather at hand to work out pattern combinations and to test moisture levels. The tools can be used to make patterns or to produce textured effects.

Lay the leather on a firm surface – marble, for example – and holding the stamp upright in one

FIG. 94 *Decorating tools*
1 *swivel knife*
2 *modellers*
3 *tracer*
4 *embosser*
5 *a selection of stamps*
6 *hide hammer*

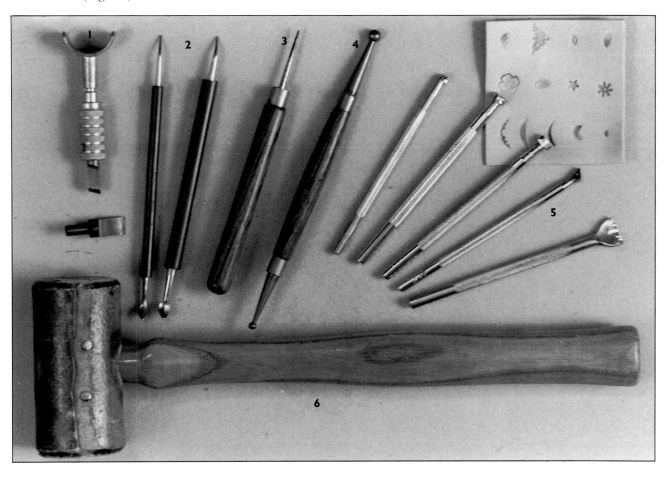

FIG. 95 *Tooling a mask with decorative stamps.*

FIG. 96 *Building up a tooled design.*

hand, strike it with a hide hammer (Fig. 95). Continue in this way, building up the design as you go (Fig. 96). Experiment by pressing objects such as coins and interesting pieces of grainy wood into the leather's surface to see what impressions they leave. When it is dry, the leather can be dyed or left natural, but it must be dressed and polished because wetting and compressing the fibres tends to make it inflexible and hard.

The more advanced decorative techniques of incising, modelling and embossing have all been well explained by others in books devoted to the subject. If you have a particular interest in developing decorative skills the titles of the most helpful books are listed on page 123.

13 *A large moulded bag, shaped using a one-piece 'last' type of mould.*

PART 3

In the chapters that follow there are 10 projects to make. The projects in Chapter 16 are for beginners; those in Chapter 17 consolidate skills already acquired and introduce some new techniques; and the projects in Chapter 18 are designed to build on and extend the skills already known and practised.

The projects have been designed to teach a range of handworking techniques so that, when you have acquired and practised the skills involved, you will be able to create your own designs. Listed at the beginning of each project are the materials and tools you will need. The step-by-step instructions are accompanied by illustrations where necessary and refer back to the relevant chapters in which the techniques are explained. Each of the finished projects is illustrated in colour.

16

BEGINNERS' PROJECTS

The first three projects involve using the basic skills, and they require only the minimum tools to complete. To make the belt and purse you will need to cut hide and skin, bevel, burnish and crease cut edges, fix a durable dot fastener and, most important of all, saddle stitch. The mask is an exercise in free-form work, an expression used to describe the manipulation and decoration of wet leather when the work can be changed during the making process. It will, perhaps, inspire further ideas for experimenting with the sculptural potential of vegetable tanned leathers.

HIDE BELT

(See colour photograph 14, page 80.)

Materials
- 3–3.5mm (8–9oz) vegetable tanned cow hide
- 40mm (1½in) brass buckle
- 3-cord no. 18 linen thread
- Beeswax
- Edge glue solution and applicator
- Edge dye and applicator
- Small piece of canvas

Tools
- Knife
- Plough gauge (optional)
- Paring knife
- No. 2 edge beveller
- Dividers
- Single creaser
- Spirit lamp
- No. 7 pricking iron
- Hide hammer
- No. 4 or 5 harness needles
- Awl – 57mm (2¼in) blade
- Stitching clam
- Revolving punch

1 If necessary, file and polish the buckle (see Chapter 14).

2 Cut a strip of hide the width of the inside diameter of the buckle and shape one end. Cut a loop 10mm wide by 85mm long (³/₈ × 3³/₈in) (see Chapter 5).

3 Pare the buckle end and the loop (see Chapter 8).

4 Bevel the edges, then dye and burnish them. Crease a line 3mm (¹/₈in) in from the edge (see Chapter 7).

5 Punch two holes and cut a slot large enough to take the buckle tongue, then mark the stitches with the pricking iron (Fig. 97).

6 Dampen and bend the leather around the buckle.

FIG. 97 *A belt end with buckle and loop.*

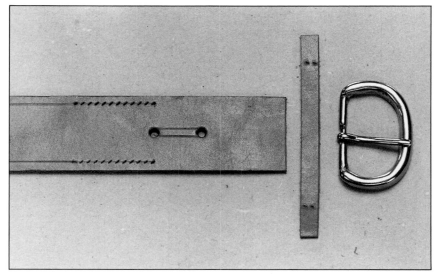

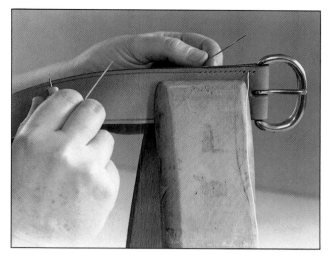

FIG. 98 *Holding the belt in a clam, ready to make a double stitch at the beginning.*

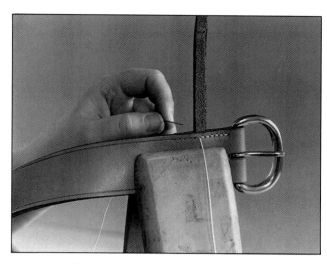

FIG. 99 *Stitching in the belt loop.*

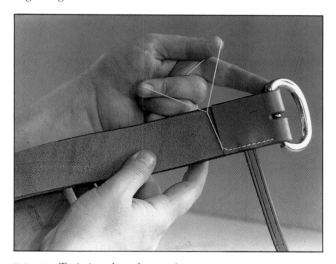

FIG. 100 *Twisting threads together across the back of a belt in preparation for stitching up the side.*

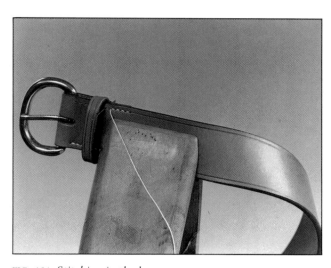

FIG. 101 *Stitching in the loop.*

7 Wax a piece of thread 80cm (32in) long and attach a harness needle to each end (see Chapter 10). With the belt held in a clam, pierce the first three holes with the awl (Fig. 98). Begin stitching in the second hole, making a double first stitch for strength. Stitch along the first side, inserting the loop at hole six (Fig. 99). Twist the two ends of thread together along the back (Fig. 100), then stitch up the second side, making sure that the loop is level (Fig. 101).

8 Finish off by stitching two holes backwards and trim both ends of thread close to the stitches on the back.

9 Use the revolving punch to make five holes slightly larger than the tongue.

14 *The hide belt and purse.*

PURSE

Materials
- 1mm (3oz) calf or pigskin
- 1.5mm (4oz) cow hide
- One baby durable dot
- 3-cord no. 18 linen thread
- Beeswax
- PVA adhesive
- Edge glue solution and applicator
- Edge dye and applicator
- Small piece of canvas

Tools
- Knife
- Dividers
- Single creaser
- Spirit lamp
- No. 7 pricking iron
- No. 5 or 4 harness needles
- Awl – 57mm (2¼in) blade
- Stitching clam
- Revolving punch
- Baby dot setter
- Hide hammer
- Scratch awl or sharp pencil
- Cork block
- Bulldog clips
- 10mm (³/₈in) flat brush

1 Draw the pattern pieces (Fig. 102) on to thin card, cut them out and draw round them. Transfer any constructional information – centres, flap position, durable dot position – on to the leather at this stage. Cut out the leather pieces (Fig. 103).

2 Dye and burnish the flap edges, then crease the curved edge only (see Chapter 7).

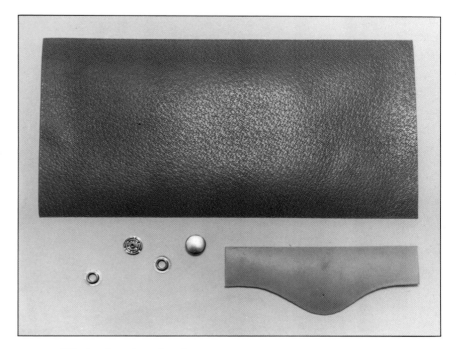

FIG. 103 *The leather pieces for the purse cut out with a durable dot.*

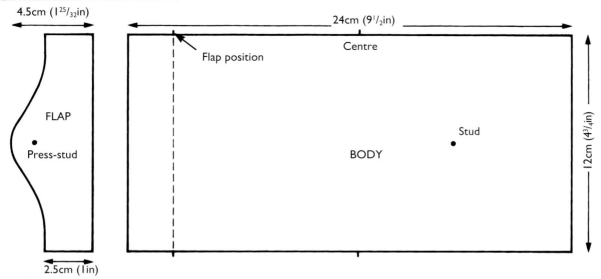

FIG. 102 *The pattern for the purse.*

4.5cm (1²⁵/₃₂in)

2.5cm (1in)

24cm (9½in)

Centre

Flap position

12cm (4³/₄in)

FLAP

Press-stud

BODY

Stud

3 Mark the stitches across the flap, 2.5mm ($^{1}/_{8}$in) from the edge.

4 Burnish the body ends.

5 Glue the flap on to the body with PVA adhesive and use an awl to pierce the stitches on the cork block.

6 Prepare a thread and, holding the work in the clam, stitch the flap in position (see Chapter 10).

7 Attach the baby durable dot (see Chapter 13).

8 Mark the body stitches 2.5mm ($^{1}/_{8}$in) from the edges down to within 2mm ($^{1}/_{16}$in) of the fold (Fig. 104).

9 Apply PVA adhesive to the side seams. Fold the body in half and hold the edges together until the glue has dried (Fig. 105).

10 Pierce the stitch marks with the awl on to a cork block, then stitch the side seams together.

11 Dye and burnish the edges.

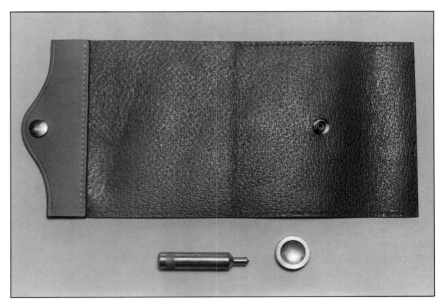

FIG. 104 *The flap and durable dot in place.*

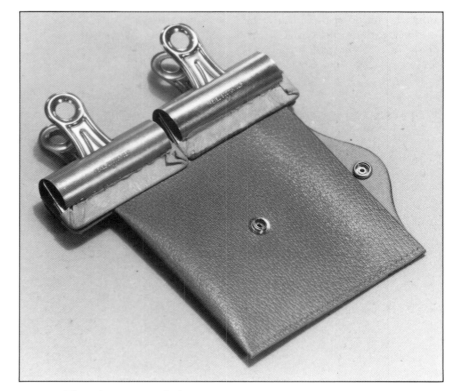

FIG. 105 *The side seams ready for stitching.*

MASK

(See colour photograph 15.)

> **Materials**
> • 1.5mm (4oz) russet belly
>
> **Tools**
> • Knife
> • Revolving punch
> • Scratch awl

1 Use the pattern (Fig. 106) or make your own by folding a sheet of paper in half. Mark the eye and nose positions, then draw a fanciful mask shape, beginning at the tip of the nose. Cut the pattern out then open it to reveal the full shape.

2 Place the pattern on the leather and hold it in position with masking-tape. Mark the outlines with a scratch awl or sharp pencil. Remove the pattern and cut out the mask (Fig. 107).

15 *Two simple moulded leather masks.*

FIG. 106 *The pattern for the mask.*

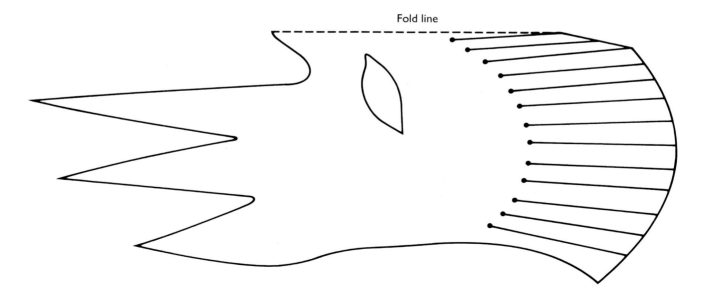

Fold line

FIG. 107 *Cutting out a mask from natural hide belly.*

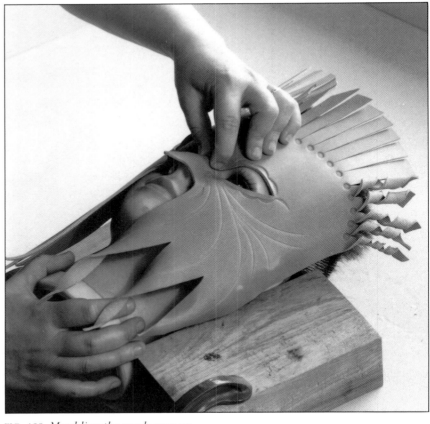

FIG. 108 *Moulding the mask over an old mannikin head.*

3 Completely submerge the mask in water for a few seconds. If you want to decorate the mask with tooling (see Chapter 15) you must do this before it is shaped. Allow the leather to dry slightly before stamping, or the tool heads will damage the leather's surface.

4 While the leather is wet, start to shape it by laying it over an old mannikin head or use your own face and a mirror. Make sure the eyes are level and in the correct position. If not, cut them larger and re-adjust the pattern for next time. Push the leather down over the bridge of the nose. This is very important in order to achieve a comfortable fit (Fig. 108).

5 Twist the strips at the top (Fig. 109) and the points at the bottom. Open out the eye holes and press the leather around the head or face to create a realistic shape. Squeeze and pull the leather in whatever way you wish to develop the mask's features.

6 You can allow the finished mask to dry naturally or you can gently 'bake' it. Place it, supported on a block of wood, in an oven set at the lowest temperature for up to two minutes. This will harden the leather. Do not let it get too hot or it will distort and shrivel.

7 When it has completely dried out, apply polish if it is to be left natural or decorate it with acrylic leather dyes.

8 If the mask is to be worn (Fig. 110), cut two strips of thong 3mm ($1/_8$in) wide and tie knots in one end. Punch a hole each side of the mask, just above ear level, and thread the thongs through.

FIG. 109 *Twisting the 'hair'.*

FIG. 110 *A mask covering a face can create a powerful image.*

17

INTERMEDIATE PROJECTS

These three projects have been designed to develop the skills already learnt – cutting out, saddle stitching and cut-edge finishing – as well as introducing new techniques and constructional ideas. To make the wallet and passport holder several layers of leather are assembled and stitched together, and a magnetic clasp is used as a closure. The folding-top bag has a shoulder strap and screw stud fastener. Both these projects are flat, so they require no gussets. The small briefcase, on the other hand, introduces a three-piece gusset to create internal space. It has a simple pocket and a flat handle, with a case lock to secure the flap.

16 *The wallet and passport holder and the folding-top bag.*

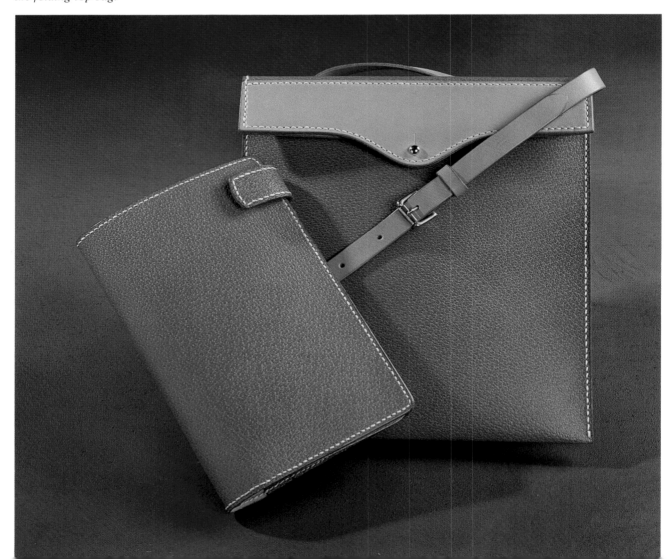

WALLET AND PASSPORT HOLDER

(See colour photograph 16.)

Materials

- 1mm (3oz) calf, goat or pig skin
- 1 small magnetic clasp
- 3-cord no. 18 linen thread
- Beeswax
- PVA adhesive
- Edge dye with applicator
- Edge glue with applicator
- Small piece of canvas

Tools

- Knife
- Paring knife
- Paring machine (optional)

- Dividers
- Single creaser
- Spirit lamp
- No. 7 pricking iron
- No. 5 harness needles
- Awl – 57mm (2¼in) blade
- Stitching clam
- Hide hammer
- Cork block
- 10mm (³/₈in) flat brush
- Bone folder
- 6 bulldog clips

1 Make accurate templates from the pattern (Fig. 111) and draw around them on the leather. Mark the positions of the pocket, divider, tab and magnetic clasp. Cut out all the pieces (Fig. 112, page 88).

2 Fix the base of the magnetic clasp into the body and the top of the clasp into the tab lining (Fig. 113, page 88). (You could use a durable dot instead.)

3 Pare the reinforcement strip by about one-third using a paring machine (see Chapter 8) or make a bevelled pare along the bottom edge with a paring knife so that when it is glued in position there will not be a pronounced ridge. Glue the reinforcement strip across the top of the wallet body. Round the top corners with a sharp knife.

4 Glue the tab to the tab lining, then mark the stitches all the way round it,

FIG. 111 *The pattern for the wallet and passport holder.*

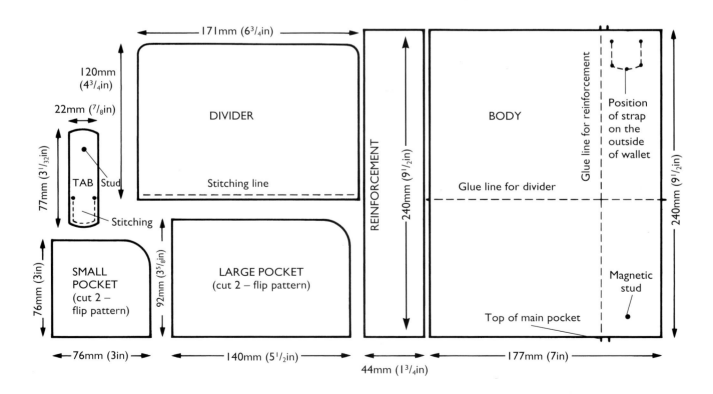

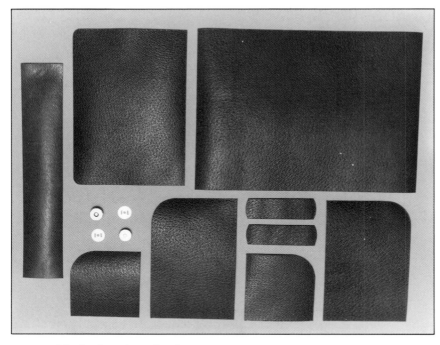

FIG. 112 *The leather pieces for the wallet and passport holder cut out and a magnetic stud fastener.*

2.5mm (¹/₈in) from the edges, and pierce them on the cork block.

5 Mark the stitches across the body so that the divider can be stitched in place.

6 On the inside of the body, mark a line where the divider must be glued in position.

7 To create a hinge on the divider, place a metal rule 6mm (¹/₄in) from the edge to be stitched and, with a bone folder, bend the leather into a right angle.

8 Dye, burnish and crease the curved pocket corners.

9 Glue the pockets in position (Fig. 114). Hold them together with bulldog clips until the glue has dried, then round the corners with a sharp knife.

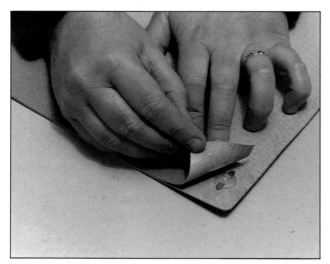

FIG. 113 *The base of the magnetic clasp is fixed to the body before the reinforcement strip is glued down.*

FIG. 114 *Gluing the pockets in place after their edges have been burnished and creased. The position of the divider has been marked on the inside.*

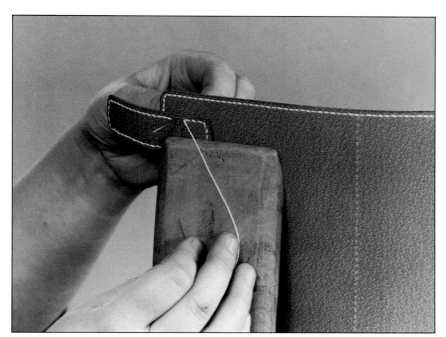

FIG. 115 *The tab being stitched to the body after the pockets have been stitched on and the edges burnished.*

FIG. 116 *Finally, the divider is stitched to the inside.*

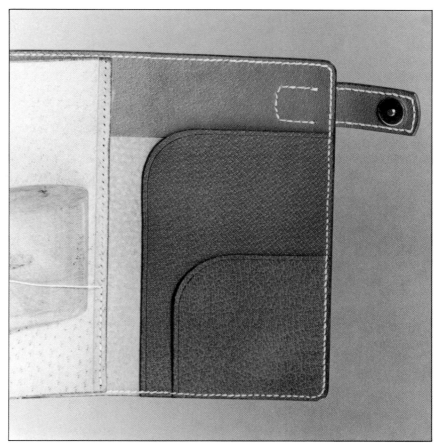

10 Use a pricking iron to mark the stitches around the body, 2.5mm (¹/₈in) in from the edges. Taking care to keep the awl upright, pierce the stitches around the wallet on a cork block.

11 Prepare a length of waxed thread and saddle stitch around the wallet.

12 Stitch the tab together, to the point at which it has to be attached to the body.

13 Dye and burnish around the edges of the wallet and tab.

14 Stitch the tab in position (Fig. 115).

15 Glue the divider to the inside of the wallet. Turn the wallet over and pierce the stitch holes through on to the cork with an awl, then stitch the divider in place (Fig. 116).

FOLDING-TOP BAG

Materials

- 1mm (3oz) calf, pig or goat skin
- 2.5mm (6oz) cow hide
- 1 brass screw stud
- 15mm ($^5/_8$in) brass buckle
- 3-cord no. 18 linen thread
- Beeswax
- Piece of canvas
- PVA adhesive
- Edge glue solution with applicator
- Edge dye with applicator

Tools

- Knife
- Clamp
- Awl – 57mm (2$^1/_4$in) blade
- Paring knife
- No. 7 pricking iron
- Hide hammer
- No. 2 edge beveller
- Revolving punch
- Size 5 or 4 harness needles
- Screw driver
- Vice (optional)
- Pliers
- Dividers
- Cork block
- Litho stone (optional)
- 10mm ($^3/_8$in) flat brush
- Bulldog clips

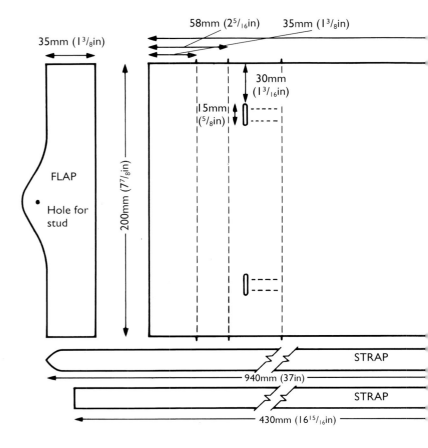

FIG. 117 *The pattern for the folding-top bag.*

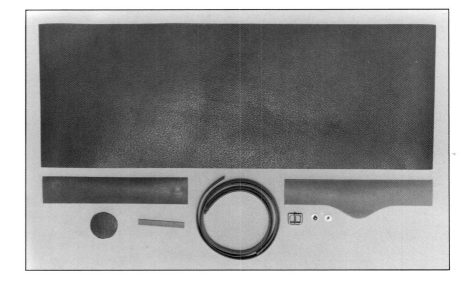

FIG. 118 *The leather pieces cut out, with the screw stud and the single-roller buckle.*

I Make templates of thin card from the drawing (Fig. 117). Lay them in position on the leather and draw around them, accurately marking important information – the stud and flap positions, the strap slots, the fold line and the position of strengthener.

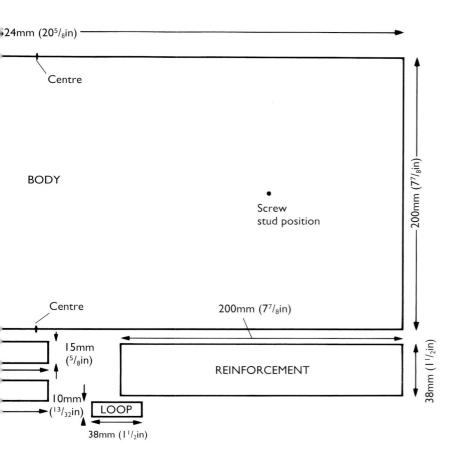

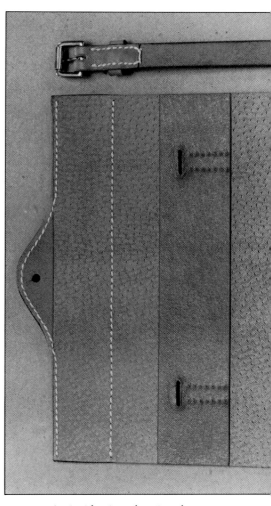

FIG. 119 *An inside view showing the flap and reinforcement strip in place, the strap slots cut and stitching holes pierced, and the buckle stitched to the shoulder strap.*

2 Cut out all the leather pieces including the strap (Fig. 118).

3 Burnish the flap end of the body, and pare and turn the other end (see Chapter 8).

4 Bevel, dye and burnish around the flap, then mark the stitches with a pricking iron, 2.5mm (^{1}/$_8$in) in from the edges.

5 Punch the hole and cut the slit in the flap.

6 Glue the flap on to the body and stitch across the back edge. Stitch across the curved front edge.

7 Glue the strengthener in position on the flesh side of the body.

8 Fix the screw stud in position (see Chapter 13) and glue the leather washer over the screw on the back.

9 If necessary, file and polish the strap buckle (see Chapter 4).

10 Bevel, dye and burnish the strap and loop.

11 Pare the strap ends that are to be stitched to the bag, and the buckle end of the strap (see Chapter 8).

12 Stitch the buckle and loop in place (see Chapter 10).

13 Cut two strap slots, making sure that they are the exact width of the strap. Mark the stitches for attaching the strap ends to the back of the bag and pierce the holes on the cork block (Fig. 119).

14 Glue, then stitch the straps in position (Fig. 120).

15 Apply glue to the edges of the body, then fold it in half. Hold the edges in position with bulldog clips until the glue has dried.

16 Pierce the stitches that are already marked on the sides of the flap, through the three layers, on to the cork. Mark the remaining stitches down each side, 2.5mm ($^1/_8$in) in from the edges and to within 2mm ($^1/_{16}$in) of the fold, and pierce these before stitching the bag together (Fig. 121).

17 If necessary, level the edges with a paring knife before dyeing and burnishing them.

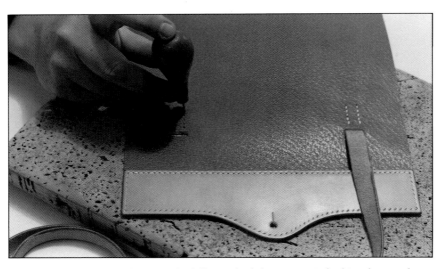

FIG. 120 *Outside view showing the billet end of the strap stitched in place and holes being pierced on the cork for the remaining strap.*

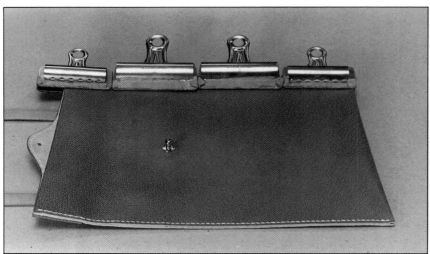

FIG. 121 *One side stitched and the other glued prior to stitching.*

SMALL BRIEF CASE

(See colour photograph 17, page 95.)

Materials
- 2.5mm (6oz) cow hide
- 1mm (3oz) calf or pig skin
- Solid brass folio lock
- 3 solid rivets
- 2 split rivets
- 2 20mm ($^3/_4$in) brass D-rings
- PVA adhesive

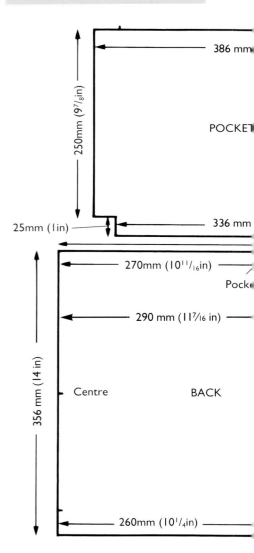

386 mm

250mm ($9^7/_8$in)

POCKET

25mm (1in)

336 mm

270mm ($10^{11}/_{16}$in)

Pock

290 mm ($11^7/_{16}$ in)

356 mm (14 in)

Centre   BACK

260mm ($10^1/_4$in)

- 4-cord no. 18 linen thread
- Beeswax
- Edge glue solution with applicator
- Edge dye with applicator
- Small piece of canvas

Tools
- Knife
- Scratch awl or pencil
- No. 7 pricking iron
- Awl – 57mm (2¼in) blade
- Size 4 harness needles
- Hide hammer
- Metal hammer

- Clam
- Pliers
- No. 2 edge beveller
- Dividers
- Single creaser
- Spirit lamp
- Bone folder
- Race
- Revolving punch
- 10mm (³⁄₈in) brush
- Bulldog clips
- Lead block (optional)
- Doming punch
- Cork block

1 Make accurate card templates from the drawings (Fig. 122).

2 Position the patterns on the leather, carefully avoiding scars, and draw around them. Transfer important constructional information – handle, gusset, pocket and lock positions – to the leather at this stage.

2 Cut out the brief-case if the leather is pre-dyed and

FIG. 122 *The pattern for the briefcase.*

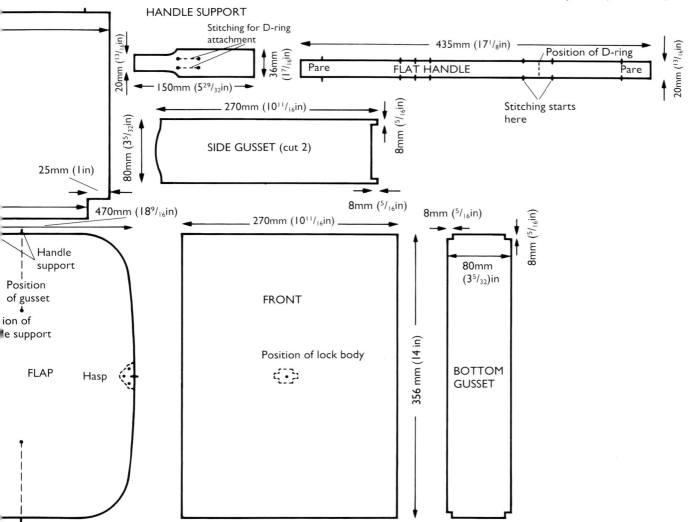

dressed. If the leather is natural, it must be finished before the pieces can be cut out (see Chapter 6).

4 Bevel, dye, burnish and crease the tops of the side gussets and the front.

5 Prepare the three-piece gusset. Dampen the flesh side of the three gusset pieces and cut channels with a race, 8mm ($1/3$in) in from the edges. Holding a straight-edge on the grain side, in the same place as the channel, firmly shape the gusset pieces into right angles with the bone folder. When the leather is dry, join the pieces together (see Chapter 11).

6 Prepare the handle. Skive a steep bevel from one end of the handle strip, starting 10mm ($3/8$in) from the end (see Chapter 8). Bevel, dye and burnish the short sections of the edges to be wrapped around the D-rings. Position the D-rings on the two fold lines, then fold the unskived section of the handle under the central section and glue it in place, using bulldog clips to hold it in position. Now fold the skived section on to this layer and glue it in place. Mark the stitching along each side of the handle and stitch the layers together. Level the edges of the stitched layers with the paring knife. Bevel, dye and burnish the edges of the handle.

7 Prepare the handle supports. Skive the ends to be wrapped around the D-rings, starting 40mm ($1^1/2$in) from the narrow ends. Bevel the grain edges only, then dye and burnish all the edges except those that are parallel with the flap. These will be finished when the flap is burnished.

Mark the stitching. Glue and stitch the ends that hold the D-rings.

8 Glue and stitch the handle supports to the case flap, working on one side at a time (Fig. 123).

9 Bevel, dye and burnish around the flap from where the gussets join the case back. Mark the stitches and stitch around the flap.

10 Attach the lock hasp in position on the flap (see Chapter 13).

11 Mark the stitches around the back and front, 3mm ($1/8$in) in from the edges.

12 Attach the lock to the case front and stitch the patch in position.

13 Burnish the pocket top and pare the sides and bottom, 6mm ($1/4$in) from the edges.

14 Glue the pocket to the case back.

15 Glue and stitch the three-piece gusset to the front, then the back.

16 Level the edges with a paring knife then bevel, dye and burnish them.

FIG. 123 *The flat handle and handle supports stitched in place.*

17 *A brief case made of tan hide.*

18

ADVANCED PROJECTS

The final four projects are all different. Each introduces the experienced maker to techniques that build on and extend the skills already known and practised. The box bag, as the name suggests, is constructed in a similar way to a hide box, so before attempting this project, learn how to box stitch by making a simple box as described in Chapter 10.

The shape of the moulded bag is formed using a two-piece wooden mould. Once the leather has been wet-moulded and dried, the bag is constructed in a similar way to any other cut-edged hide bag.

To make the quilted belt a decorative pattern is stitched through two layers of calf, with raw fleece caught between them to form a padded area. The edges are pared and turned, and the buckle is covered in leather and stitched. The effect is a delicate, soft belt that looks comfortable to wear.

The last project, the large shoulder bag, has a turnover bound-edge construction. It has U-shaped gussets, a linen lining and a hanging pocket, and a buckle is used to secure the flap. It illustrates how the careful selection of material to take account of the type of construction can create a practical, lightweight bag that is both strong and stylish.

BOX BAG

Materials
- 2.5mm (6oz) cow hide, preferably from the butt
- Scrap of 1mm (3oz) skin
- 3 brass screw studs
- 4-cord no. 18 linen thread
- Beeswax
- Small piece of canvas
- Edge dye and applicator
- Edge glue and applicator
- Rubber solution
- Wooden block or laminated board

Tools
- Scratch awl or sharp pencil
- Knife
- No. 7 pricking iron
- No. 4 harness needles
- Hide hammer
- Awl – 57mm (2¼in) blade
- Dividers
- Single creaser
- Spirit lamp
- No. 2 edge beveller
- Revolving punch
- Screw driver
- Pliers
- Vice (optional)
- Cork block
- 6 strong rubber bands

1 Begin by making a stitching block from a piece of inexpensive wood or laminated board. Make it at least 10mm ($^3/_8$in) deeper than the depth of the gusset. Smooth the surfaces with sandpaper but do not round off the edges.

2 Make card templates from the drawing (Fig. 124), carefully position them on the leather and cut out the pieces. Cut the strap. Be sure to mark the stud positions, centres and the exact points where the gusset is stitched to the back.

3 Bevel, dye, burnish and crease around the flap, the tops of the gusset and the front and the strap.

4 Bevel only the grain edges of the back and front, then dye and burnish them. Leave the sides of the gusset raw.

5 Prepare the bag for box stitching by marking the stitches 3mm ($^1/_8$in) in from the edges around the front, back and the gusset sides. Pierce the gusset stitches on the cork block, holding the awl at an angle (see Chapter 10).

18 (right) *Box bags.*

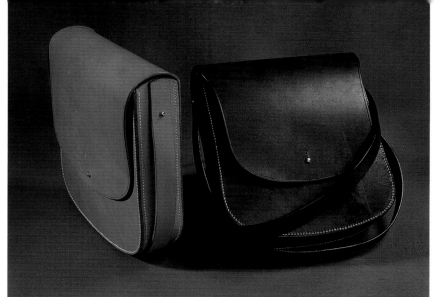

FIG. 124 (below) *The pattern for the box bag.*

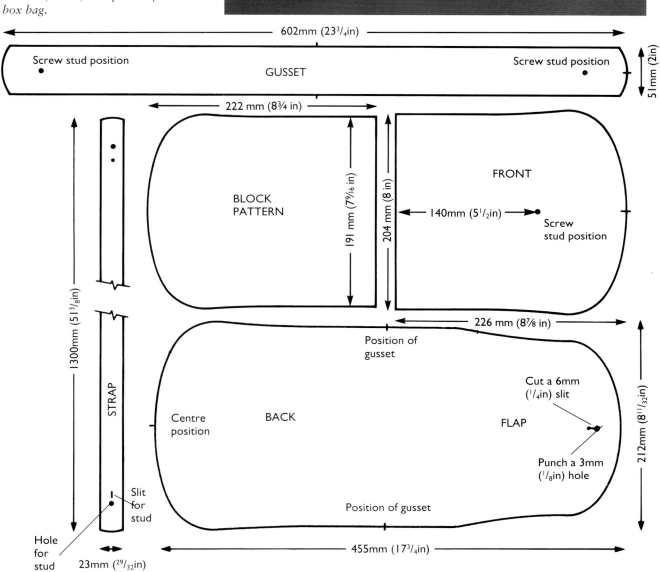

602mm (23³/₄in)

Screw stud position   GUSSET   Screw stud position

51mm (2in)

222 mm (8³/₄ in)

BLOCK PATTERN

191 mm (7⁹/₁₆ in)

204 mm (8 in)

FRONT

140mm (5¹/₂in)   Screw stud position

226 mm (8⁷/₈ in)

Position of gusset

1300mm (51³/₈in)

STRAP

BACK

Centre position

FLAP

Cut a 6mm (¹/₄in) slit

Punch a 3mm (¹/₈in) hole

212mm (8¹¹/₃₂in)

Position of gusset

Slit for stud

Hole for stud

23mm (²⁹/₃₂in)

455mm (17³/₄in)

6 Mark the stud washer stitches on the front.

7 Fix the screw studs into position on the gusset (see Chapter 13).

8 Carefully apply rubber solution to the raw edge of one side of the gusset and close to the edge on the flesh side of the front.

9 With the grain side of the front flat on the bench, lay the block in position. Glue the gusset at a right angle to the front, starting in the centre and using the block for support. Hold the pieces in place with strong rubber bands until you have begun stitching.

10 Prepare two threads and begin box stitching (Fig. 125).

11 As you stitch you will notice that the stitch marks on the gusset and bag front become misaligned. This is because the gusset stitches have further to travel. To level the stitches up it is necessary to lose a stitch by making two stitches into the same hole on the front while travelling two stitches along the gusset. Do this by piercing the misaligned holes with the awl, then, with the tip of the awl in the same hole on the front, pierce the hole level with it on the gusset – that is, make one hole in the front but two in the gusset. Make the first stitch normally. Now push the left needle through the left hole in the gusset and into the parallel, but already used, hole in the front (Fig. 126). Pull the left needle through, using pliers if you need to, then push the right needle through the same route (Fig. 127). Carefully pull the stitches tight. The 'lost' stitch should disappear just below the surface of the front. Repeat this procedure as often as you need to keep the stitching holes aligned.

12 Once the front and gusset have been stitched together, punch a hole and fix the screw stud into the front (see Chapter 13). Glue the washer in place on the flesh side of the front to cover the screw, and stitch it in place. The washer will provide support when the flap is pushed on to the stud.

13 Glue the back and gusset together with rubber solution.

14 Stitch them together, using a small block of wood inside the bag to give support wherever necessary.

15 Punch holes and cut short slits in the flap and strap ends so that they fit over the screw studs (Fig. 128).

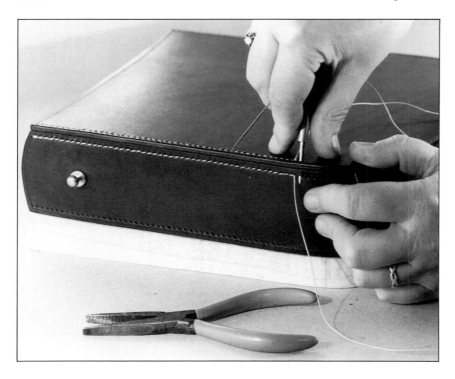

FIG. 125 *Box stitching on the block.*

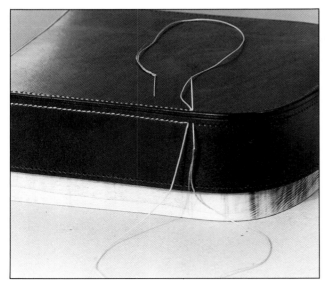

FIG. 126 *Losing a stitch – the path of the left needle.*

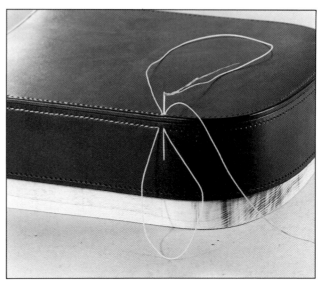

FIG. 127 *Losing a stitch – the path of the right needle.*

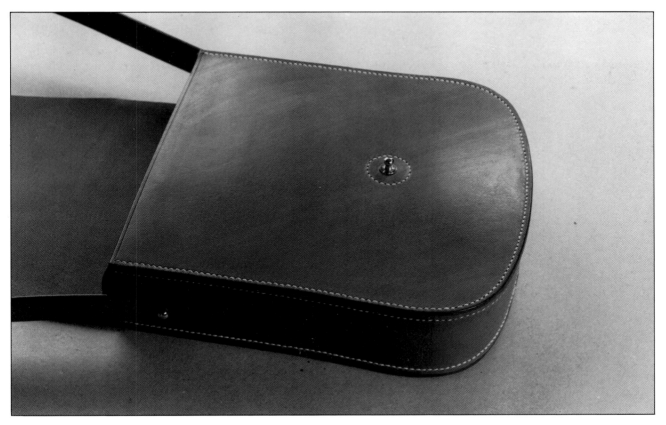

FIG. 128 *The strap ends attached to screw studs on the gusset.*

MOULDED SHOULDER BAG

(See colour photograph 19. Before the bag can be constructed, you must make a two-piece wooden mould.)

MATERIALS AND TOOLS FOR MOULD

- A block of pine or similar wood, $38 \times 226 \times 185$mm ($1^{1}/_{2} \times 8^{3}/_{4} \times 7^{1}/_{4}$in)
- A piece of chipboard $16 \times 300 \times 340$mm ($^{5}/_{8} \times 11^{3}/_{4} \times 13^{1}/_{4}$in)
- A piece of plywood $18 \times 300 \times 340$mm ($^{2}/_{3} \times 11^{3}/_{4} \times 13^{1}/_{4}$in)
- 25mm (1in) screws
- Medium and fine sandpaper
- Wood-working tools

1 Using the mould pattern (Fig. 129), cut the block of pine to size and shape.

2 Draw the curved profile on to each side of the mould top. With a plane, begin to shape the wood, using a shaped cardboard profile to check the shape.

3 Use a rasp to remove sharp angles. You need to create a smooth, continuous curve from the flat face of the mould to the sides. Finish off with sandpaper until the wood feels completely smooth.

4 Mark the position of the mould centrally on the chipboard. On the back, drill four screw holes, countersink them and screw the mould to the chipboard.

5 Cut a window from the middle of the plywood to make the mould top. The window should be larger than the mould by 3mm ($^{1}/_{8}$in) all round, except at the top, to allow for the thickness of the leather.

6 Strengthen the straight edge along the top of the mould with a strip of plywood.

7 Seal the bare wood with French polish or shellac. The two-piece mould is now ready to use.

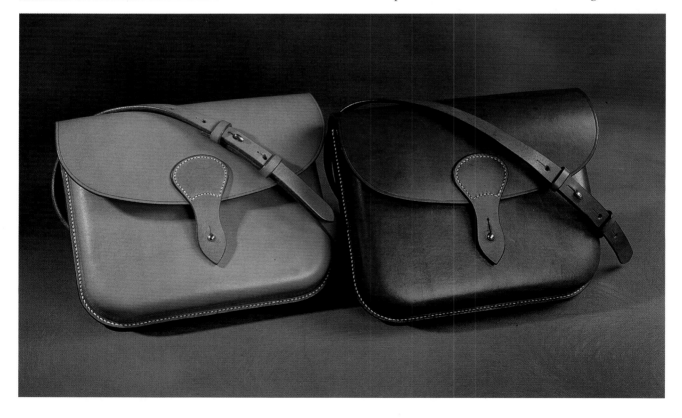

19 *Moulded shoulder bags.*

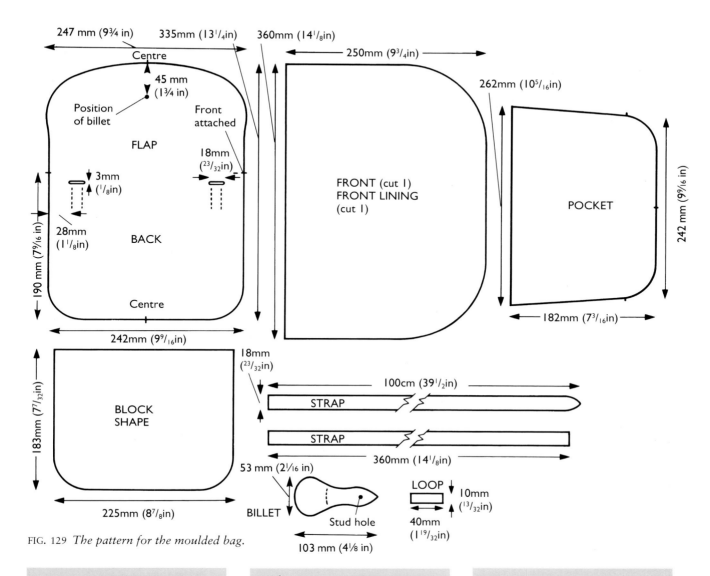

FIG. 129 *The pattern for the moulded bag.*

MATERIALS AND TOOLS FOR BAG

Materials
- 2–2.5mm (5–6oz) cow hide
- 0.5–1.0mm (1–3oz) pig or calf skin
- Screw stud
- 18mm (³/₄in) buckle
- 4-cord no. 18 linen thread
- Edging glue with applicator
- Edging dye with applicator
- PVA adhesive
- Beeswax

- Pliantene or 4-Way Care
- Neutral shoe cream
- Piece of canvas

Tools
- Knife
- Dividers
- No. 7 pricking iron
- No. 4 harness needles
- Bone folder
- Pliers
- Scratch awl
- Revolving punch
- Paring knife
- No. 2 edge beveller

- Single creaser
- Spirit lamp
- Awl – 57mm (2¹/₄in) blade
- Clam
- Bulldog clips
- 8 G-cramps
- 57mm (2¹/₄in) crew punch (optional)
- 10mm (³/₈in) brush

Make card patterns from the drawing (Fig. 129). Position and draw around them on to the leather, making sure that you mark the positions of the stud, strap and billet. Cut the front to be moulded from an area of leather near to the shoulder or middle of the hide, not from the butt end. Cut out all the pieces, including the strap.

2 Submerge the front in warm water (Fig. 130) until it is completely saturated (Fig. 131). With the grain side facing upwards, lay it centrally on the mould and make sure that the top is level with the top of the mould. Use small brass or steel tacks to fix the leather close to the sides at the top of the mould but outside the cutting allowance to prevent any movement when the mould top is laid over and held (Fig. 132). Push the leather down around the mould (Fig. 133) and remove V-shaped pieces of excess leather to help the mould top to lie flat (Fig. 134). Lay the mould top over the leather, and firmly and evenly press it down (Fig. 135). Attach G-cramps, placing them opposite one another until the mould is completely surrounded. Once the G-cramps are in place, gradually tighten them, carefully balancing the pressure applied on each side of the mould (Fig. 136). Allow the leather to dry naturally, or you could use a hair-dryer to speed things up.

FIG. 130 *Submerging the front of the bag in water.*

FIG. 131 *The leather saturated with water.*

FIG. 132 *The front is tacked to the mould base.*

FIG. 133 *Use the sides of your hands to form the leather around the mould.*

FIG. 134 *V-shaped darts are cut to allow the leather to be pressed flat.*

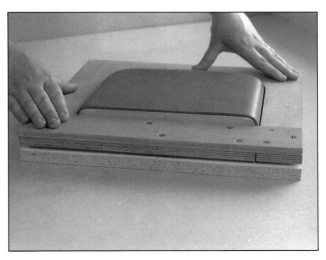

FIG. 135 *The mould top is pressed evenly down over the base.*

FIG. 136 *Evenly spaced G-cramps hold the mould in place until the leather is dry.*

3 When the leather feels dry, which can take up to 24 hours, remove the mould top but leave the leather in position a little longer to allow the sides to dry out completely. Carefully loosen and remove the side tacks (Fig. 137).

4 Set your dividers to 5mm (1/4in) and mark a cutting line around the mould (Fig. 138).

5 Keeping the knife upright, cut away the excess leather (Fig. 139).

6 Mark the stitches 3mm (1/8in) in from this edge and across the front top, which will have shrunk into a smooth curve. Apply a coat of Pliantene or polish, then remove the leather from the mould.

7 Punch a hole and attach the screw stud in the front (see Chapter 13).

8 Wet-mould the lining in the same way but with the grain side facing downwards.

9 When the lining is dry, place the front over it and trim the lining to size. Make a bevelled pare all around the curved edges of the lining, 6mm (1/4in) in, and glue it to the front with PVA adhesive.

10 Stitch across the top of the front, then bevel, dye and burnish this edge.

11 Bevel, dye and burnish around the flap, straps and billet.

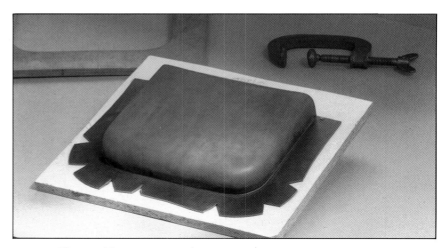

FIG. 137 *The mould top is removed when the leather is dry.*

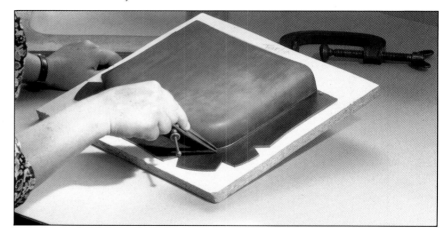

FIG. 138 *Mark the cutting line with dividers set at 5mm (1/4in).*

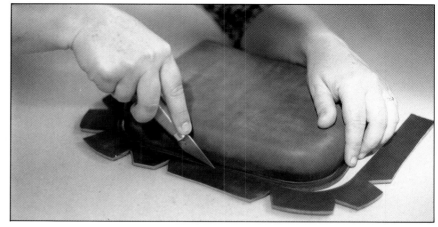

FIG. 139 *Cut away the excess leather.*

12 Cut the strap slots in the bag and mark the stitches. Mark stitches around the billet. Crease the flap (Fig. 140).

13 Punch a 3mm ($^1/_8$in) hole and 6mm ($^1/_4$in) slit in the billet. Glue and stitch it to the bag (Fig. 141).

14 Attach the buckle to the short length of strap, in the same way as a belt buckle is attached (see Chapter 16).

15 Bevel and pare the strap ends, then glue them to the bag through the slots.

16 Prepare the pocket by burnishing, or paring and turning the top edge (see Chapter 8). From 6mm ($^1/_4$in) in, pare the edges to be stitched in with the main seam. Glue the pocket to the inside of the back.

17 With the aid of bulldog clips, glue the moulded front and back together, then stitch them, using an awl with a long blade to avoid damaging the front.

18 Once stitched, level the edge with a paring knife. Now bevel, dye and burnish it.

19 Polish the finished bag.

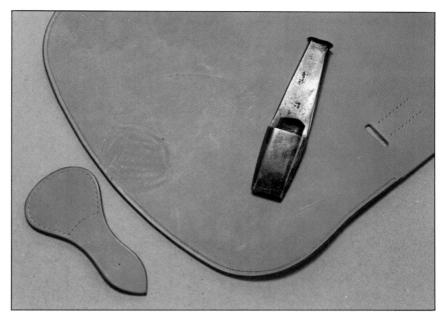

FIG. 140 *A crew punch can be used to make the strap slot.*

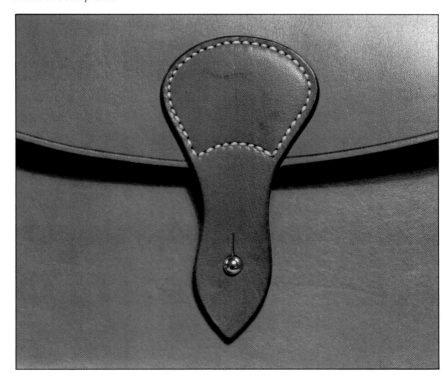

FIG. 141 *The billet is stitched to the bag flap and pressed in place over the stud to check that the hole and slit are the correct size.*

QUILTED BELT

(See colour photographs 20, page 108 and 21, page 109.)

Materials
- 0.5–0.75mm (1–2oz) calf skin
- 16mm ($^5/_8$in) half-buckle
- 2 reels silk buttonhole thread or 3-cord no. 35 linen thread
- Size 6 or 7 harness needles
- Raw sheep's fleece
- PVA adhesive
- Beeswax

Tools
- Knife
- Paring knife
- Paring machine (optional)
- Strop
- Scratch awl or sharp pencil
- Dividers
- No. 10 and 12 pricking irons
- Hide hammer
- Awl – 45mm (1$^3/_4$in) or 51mm (2in) blade
- Revolving punch
- 10mm ($^3/_8$in) brush
- Cork block
- 6 bulldog clips
- Wool carders (optional)
- Litho stone (optional)

1 Make the patterns for the body and lining to fit the required waist size – that is, add 175mm (6$^3/_4$in) to your waist measurement (Fig. 142). Mark around the two patterns on the leather, making sure that the body is on the best area of the skin. The lining should be from the same leather, but it does not have to be perfect, although it must be firm.

2 Turn the lining pattern over and use it as the turning pattern. Lay it on the flesh side of the body and use a fine pen to mark the turn line all round. Make a steep pare from this line to the edge (see Chapter 8). The belt tip turnover must be pared thinly so that it gathers up and presses flat when the lining is attached.

3 Accurately glue down the turnover using the turning pattern to help give a crisp edge (see Chapter 9). Use the top of the bone folder to make tiny pleats around the belt tip.

4 Use a no. 10 pricking iron to mark the stitches around the belt body to within 45mm (1$^3/_4$in) of each side of the buckle end and 2.5mm ($^1/_8$in) in from the edge.

5 Transfer the quilting design to a piece of tracing-paper and hold it in position on the bench with masking-tape. Slide the leather underneath the tracing-paper. Use a blunt point to draw over the design lines so that an impression is left on the leather. Remove the tracing pattern.

6 Mark the stitches of the design with a no. 12 pricking iron. Take care to mark a stitch wherever two lines meet or cross and tip the tool to one side, using only two or three teeth around curves (Fig. 143).

7 Apply PVA adhesive to all areas of the body except the section to be quilted; apply a 5mm ($^3/_{16}$in) band of glue to the top edge only. Glue the lining in place.

8 On the cork, pierce the quilting stitches through the

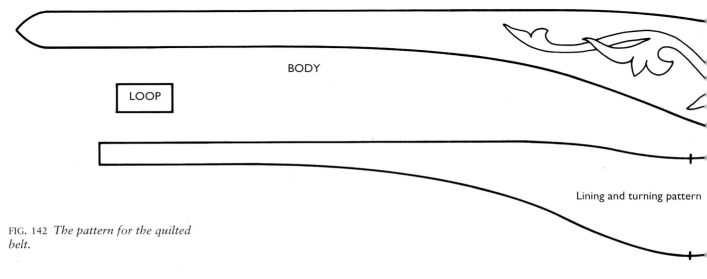

BODY

LOOP

Lining and turning pattern

FIG. 142 *The pattern for the quilted belt.*

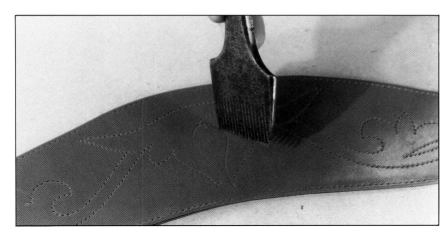

FIG. 143 *Tipping the pricking iron to one side around small curves.*

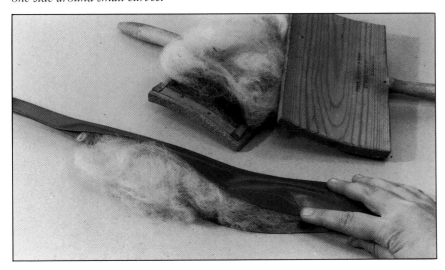

two layers of leather, keeping the awl upright. This takes a long time so be sure to keep the piercing as accurate as possible.

9 Tease out the raw fleece and remove any lumps or bits, using wool carders or your fingers. A local handspinner might do this for you. Once you have three or four rolls of fibres, begin to lay them between the belt layers. You will need much more in the centre, tapering out to the sides. It is surprising how much the wool compresses, so be sure to use plenty (Fig. 144). When you are satisfied that there are even quantities on each side of the centre, apply a 5mm ($^3/_{16}$in) wide band of glue to the bottom edges and hold them together with bulldog clips until the glue is dry.

10 Pierce the stitches around the belt on the cork, leaving those to be used for attaching the buckle. Stitch the edges of the belt but leave 200mm (8in) across the bottom

FIG. 144 (left) *Positioning the fleece after it has been carded.*

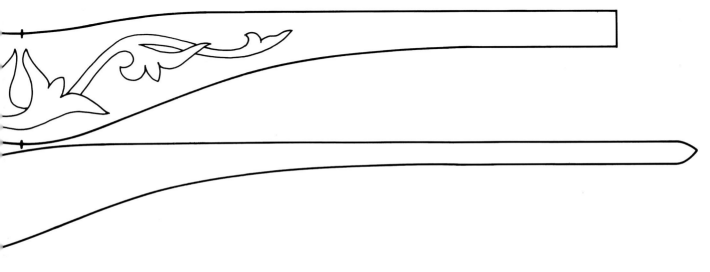

centre area unstitched, in case you have to add more fleece.

11 You will need to make many short lengths of silk thread, but begin by preparing six. Stitch in the usual way, gently pulling the stitches together. Always start and finish at a junction. Use a very sharp knife or a pair of tiny scissors to cut off the thread ends on the back. Now that there is fleece between the two layers of leather, locating the corresponding holes in each piece has to be done very carefully. If the quilting begins to look thin, gently part the glued bottom edges and add more fleece without disturbing the fibres already laid.

12 If you wish, the buckle can be covered with matching leather and stitched (see Chapter 13).

13 Pare the loop so that the sides fold neatly into the centre back. Mark and stitch a row of stitches along each edge.

14 Attach the buckle (Fig. 145) and punch the adjusting holes.

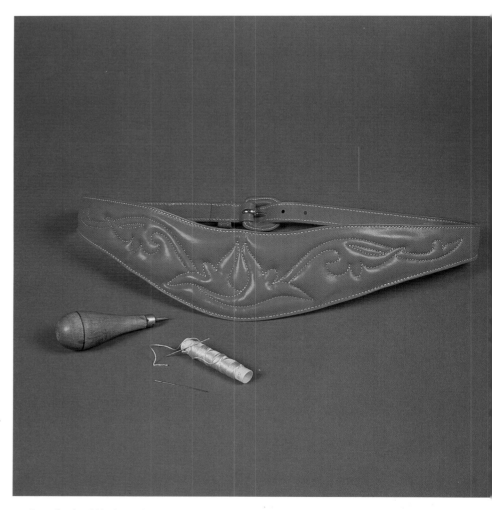

20 *A quilted calf belt with a leather-covered buckle.*

FIG. 145 *The leather-covered buckle and the loop stitched into place.*

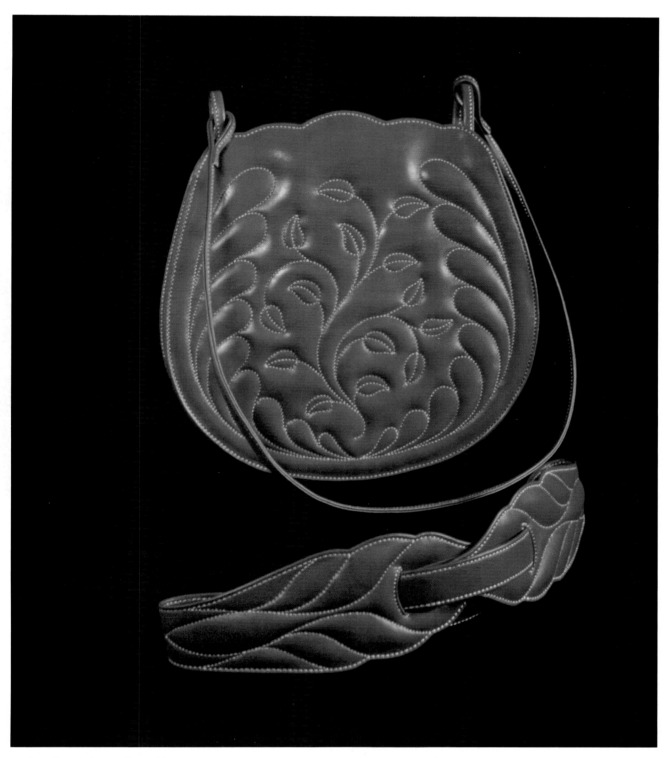

21 *A quilted belt together with a
quilted bag.*

LARGE SHOULDER BAG

(See colour photograph 22, page 112.)

Materials
- 1–1.5mm (3–4oz) calf or goat skin
- 2mm (5oz) cow hide
- Natural linen
- 2 25mm (1in) brass buckles
- 2 25mm (1in) brass D-rings
- 3-cord no. 18 linen thread
- PVA adhesive
- Edging glue and applicator
- Edging canvas

Tools
- Knife
- Strop
- Paring knife
- Paring machine (optional)
- Awl – 57mm (2¼in) blade
- Size 5 harness needles
- Cork block
- Clam
- Bone folder
- Steel rule
- Single creaser
- Spirit lamp
- No. 7 pricking iron
- Hide hammer
- Bulldog clips
- 10mm (³/₈in) brush

1 Make card patterns from the drawing (Fig. 146).

2 Cut the body, gussets, pocket and reinforcement from the skin. Cut the flap, shoulder strap, strap ends, billet, D-ring holder, buckle holder and support from the hide. The lining is cut from linen.

3 Pare the turning allowances at the ends of the body ready for turning. Pare the

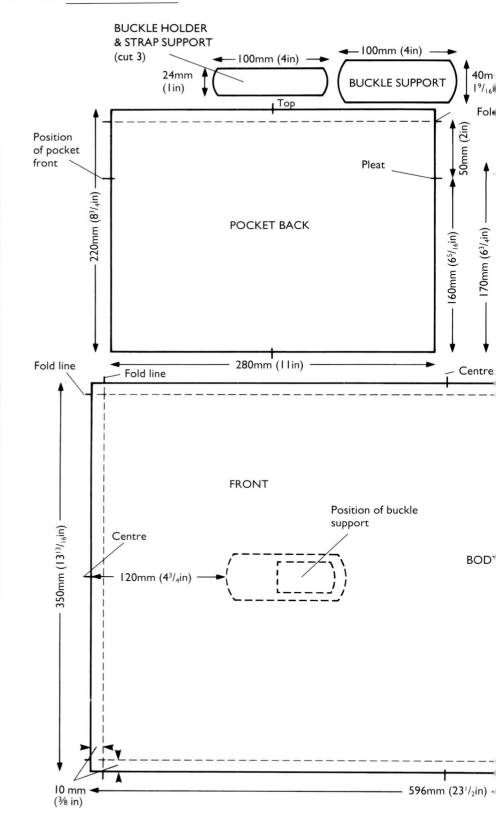

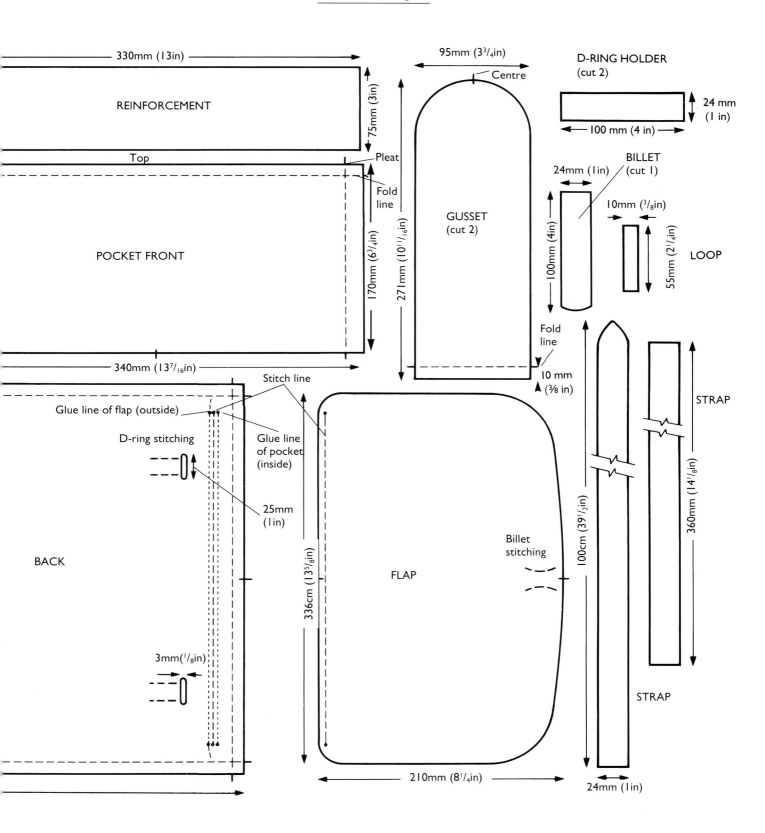

REINFORCEMENT

330mm (13in)

75mm (3in)

Top

Pleat

Fold line

POCKET FRONT

170mm (6³/₄in)

340mm (13⁷/₁₆in)

95mm (3³/₄in)

Centre

GUSSET (cut 2)

271mm (10¹¹/₁₆in)

Fold line

10 mm (³/₈ in)

D-RING HOLDER (cut 2)

24 mm (1 in)

100 mm (4 in)

24mm (1in)

BILLET (cut 1)

100mm (4in)

10mm (³/₈in)

55mm (2¹/₄in)

LOOP

STRAP

Stitch line

Glue line of flap (outside)

D-ring stitching

Glue line of pocket (inside)

25mm (1in)

BACK

3mm (¹/₈in)

336cm (13⁵/₈in)

FLAP

Billet stitching

100cm (39¹/₂in)

360mm (14¹/₈in)

210mm (8¹/₄in)

24mm (1in)

STRAP

111

22 *The large shoulder bag.*

turnover binding allowances along the sides of the body, by about one-third of their thickness.

4 Glue the reinforcement strip to the flesh side of the body back.

5 Cut the strap slots and mark the short lines of stitching ready for attaching the D-ring holders.

6 Prepare the gussets by paring the turning allowances at the tops and gluing them down. On the flesh side, dampen around the U-shaped edges. Make a heavy card moulding pattern and shape the gussets using a bone folder (see Chapter 11).

7 Prepare the pocket. Pare the turning allowances at the top of the pocket back and front, then glue them down. Pare the pleated area at each side of the front at the bottom. Form the pleats with a bone folder and metal ruler. Glue the pocket sides together and stitch. Now glue and stitch the bottom, carefully forming the side pleats. Burnish the cut edges (Fig. 147).

8 Prepare the flap. Edge bevel and burnish it. Mark the stitches across the back and crease the remaining edges. Edge bevel, burnish and crease the billet. Mark the stitches for attaching it to the flap, then glue it in place. Pierce the stitching holes on the cork then stitch.

9 Skive the buckle holder down to about 1.5mm ($^1/_{16}$in) and cut a slot for the buckle tongue. Glue it together by folding it in half so that the buckle

FIG. 147 *A side view of the pleated pocket stitched in place.*

FIG. 148 *Gluing D-ring holders in position through the slots. Stitches are marked across the back of the flap, and the billet is glued in place ready for stitching.*

is sandwiched between, then bevel and burnish the edges. Mark the stitches, 3mm ($^1/_8$in) in from the edge. Edge bevel and burnish the buckle support and mark the stitches around the edge. Glue, then stitch the buckle holder to the support. Also glue, then stitch the support to the bag body front. This will be easier to do if the holes are pierced on the cork before stitching.

10 Prepare the D-ring holders by skiving them just enough so that they can be easily folded in half with the D-rings caught between. Glue them to the inside of the body, through the slots. Pierce the holes, then stitch them in place (Fig. 148).

11 Glue one end of the linen lining to an end of the body along the fold line. Glue the turning allowance on to it and stitch it in place, 3mm ($^1/_8$in) from the edge. Do the same at the other end (Fig. 149).

12 Glue the flap to the body and pierce the holes. On the inside, position and glue the pocket so that the same row of stitching also stitches the pocket in place. Pierce the holes again, this time making holes across the pocket top only. Now stitch the three layers together (Fig. 150).

13 Prepare the strap. Edge bevel and burnish the strap ends, the two-piece strap and the loop. Mark the stitches around one side of each strap end. Attach the buckle by cutting a slot for the tongue and stitching it in place in the same way as a belt buckle is attached (see Chapter 16). Glue

FIG. 149 *The turning allowance being glued down over the linen lining at the front end of the bag body.*

FIG. 150 *A view of the inside, showing the line of stitching that attaches the pocket and flap to the bag.*

the strap ends to one side of the strap and pierce the holes. Pass them through the D-rings, glue, then stitch them in place (Fig. 151).

14 Find, or make, a short length of card tubing with a large enough diameter to support the body of the bag while the lining is glued in place. Apply a narrow strip of glue along the inside of the fold line of the turnover binding down each side and attach the lining at the very edges only.

15 The gussets can now be glued in place in two stages, one at a time. Once the PVA adhesive holding the lining has dried, apply glue to the shaped gusset lip. Beginning at the centre, glue in the gusset, following the fold line and keeping the edge of the gusset flush with the edge of the lining. When it is dry, glue the turnover binding to the gusset, covering the raw edges. Use the tip of the bone folder to make tiny pleats when you cover the curved U shape (Fig. 152). Hold the binding in place with bulldog clips until the glue has dried.

16 Carefully mark the stitches 3mm ($^1/_8$in) from the edge. They can be pierced before stitching, but if you pierce them as you go, you can adjust where the awl tip emerges on the back with greater accuracy, especially if you have marked a guideline with your dividers.

FIG. 151 *The strap ends being attached to the D-rings.*

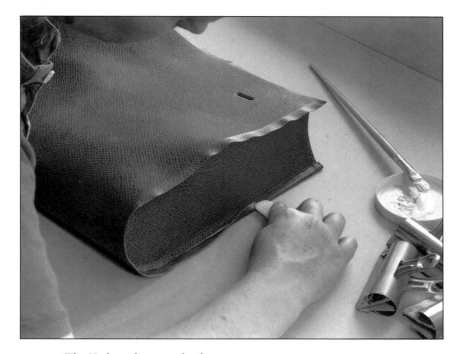

FIG. 152 *The U-shaped gusset glued to the body along the fold line. The turnover binding is glued to the gusset before stitching.*

GLOSSARY

Most of these terms and descriptions refer to vegetable tanned leathers as used throughout this book.

Back The main area of a hide less the two bellies (*q.v.*).

Belly The weakest area of the hide, which would have covered the underside of the animal.

Bevelling The process of removing thin shavings from the edges of leather before burnishing (*q.v.*).

Binding A strip of leather used to wrap around raw edges to protect them.

Buffing The removal by an abrasive of the top surface from the grain of a piece of leather to eliminate scars and surface scratches; also known as snuffing.

Burnishing The process of polishing the cut edges of leather with a gum solution or of polishing the leather's surface with a smooth piece of boxwood.

Butt The best area of a hide with the bellies (*q.v.*) and shoulder removed.

Carving The (misleading) term used to describe the use of decorative cuts in the surface of damp leather, usually an outline of a pattern, which can then be developed by modelling and tooling (*qq.v.*).

Case hide A firm hide, prepared for luggage and bag makers.

Channelling The process of using a tool known as a race to cut a narrow V- or U-shaped groove from either surface of a piece of leather to facilitate bending.

Creasing The process of impressing a thin, decorative line into the surface of the grain, usually close to the edge, with a heated tool.

Cut-edged work The name given to leather goods that are made with the edges of the leather left raw (not turned) and finished by being burnished (*q.v.*) to a hard shine.

Embossing The term used to describe an all-over texture or pattern impressed into the surface of the leather. It is also used to describe the method of decorating leather when a design is made to stand out in relief by exerting pressure from the flesh side (*q.v.*).

Flesh side The fibrous underside of leather.

Full grain The original top surface of the leather, without any buffing (*q.v.*).

Hide The whole skin of a large animal (cow, ox, horse and so on).

Incising The process of cutting a design into the surface of damp leather; more commonly, but less accurately, known as carving (*q.v.*).

Modelling The term used to describe a form of surface decoration that impresses a design in low relief without cutting.

Moulding The process of manipulating wet leather, with or without the aid of moulds, to create three-dimensional forms or relief.

Paring The process of reducing the thickness of skin from the flesh side.

Quilting The term used to describe the decorative stitching used to hold padding (sheep's fleece, for example) in place.

Racing Another term for channelling (*q.v.*).

Rounding The process of wrapping leather around a core and stitching it to form a cylindrical strap or handle.

Russet The name given to vegetable tanned hide that has been left in its natural state so that it can be used for decorative work.

Side The name given to half a hide (*q.v.*).

Skin The leather from a small animal (calf, pig, goat and so on); c.f. hide.

Skiving The process of reducing the thickness of a hide over a small area from the flesh side.

Snuffing Another term for buffing (*q.v.*).

Splitting The process of reducing the thickness of a piece of leather over a large area.

Stamping The process of decorating the surface of natural leather by impressing it with 'stamps'; also known as tooling.

Tooling Another term for stamping (*q.v.*).

Turned edges The process of turning a leather edge back on itself rather than leaving it raw.

Vegetable tanned The name given to leather made from tanning agents such as tree barks, leaves and other vegetable materials.

SUPPLIERS

(M = manufacturer; W = wholesaler; R = retailer; C = catalogue; LQ = large quantity; SQ = small quantities)

UK

ADHESIVES

PVA adhesive
Interlock Adhesives Ltd., Interlock House, Hospital Site, Hill End Road, Harefield, Middlesex UB9 6JH (tel: 0895 825911) (M)

Rubber solution
F. Ball & Co. Ltd, Barnsfield Industrial Estate, Leek, Staffordshire ST13 5QH (M)

BOOKBINDING SUPPLIES

Bone folders, PVA adhesive, paring knives, pigskin
Hewit & Son Ltd, Unit 28, Park Royal Metro Centre, Britannia Way, off Coronation Road, London NW10 7PR (tel: 081 965 5377) (M, SQ, LQ)

DYES AND FINISHES

J.T. Batchelor, 9–10 Culford Mews, London N1 4DZ (tel: 071 254 2962) (R, SQ, C)
Pearce Tandy Ltd, Billing Park, Wellingborough Road, Northampton NN3 4BG (tel: 0604 407177) (R, C)

Pliantene
Conservation Resources (UK) Ltd, Unit 1 Pony Road, Horspath Industrial Estate, Cowley, Oxon OX4 2RD (tel: 0865 747755) (SQ)

GENERAL SUPPLIERS

Tools, threads, dyes, beeswax, buckles, fittings, etc.
Abbey Saddlery, Marlborough Close, Parkgate Industrial Estate, Knutsford, Cheshire WA16 8NF (tel: 0565 65 0343) (W, SQ, C)
J.T. Batchelor, 9–10 Culford Mews, London N1 4DZ (tel: 071 254 2962) (R, SQ, C)
S. Glassner, 476 Kingston Road, Raynes Park, London SW20 8DX (tel: 081 543 1666) (SQ)
Pearce Tandy Ltd, Billing Park, Wellingborough Road, Northampton NN3 4BG (tel: 0604 407177) (R, C)

VEGETABLE TANNED LEATHERS

Oak bark hide, natural, or coloured and dressed
J. & F.J. Baker & Co. Ltd, The Tannery, Colyton, Devon (tel: 0297 52282) (M, SQ)

Hide
J.T. Batchelor, 9–10 Culford Mews, London N1 4DZ (tel: 071 254 2962) (R, SQ, C)
Hooper & Hucker Ltd, 52 Short Acre Street, Walsall, West Midlands WS2 8HW (tel: 0922 23639) (SQ)

Calf and kid skins
J.R. Tusting & Co. Ltd, 29–31 Olney Road, Lavendon, Bucks (tel: 0234 712266) (W, SQ)

Calf
Odell, Wilston & Tilt, Gladstone Road, Northampton (tel: 0604 750740) (M, LQ)

Pigskin
Hewit & Son Ltd, Unit 28, Park Royal Metro Centre, Britannia Way, off Coronation Street, London NW10 7PR (tel: 081 965 5377) (M, SQ, LQ)

GENERAL LEATHER MERCHANTS

A. & A. Crack, 18 Henry Street, Northampton (tel: 0604 232135) (W, SQ)
A.W. Midgley & Son Ltd, Combe Batch, Wedmore, Somerset (tel: 09343 712837) (W, SQ)

LININGS

Leather
J.R. Tusting & Co. Ltd, 29–31 Olney Road, Lavendon, Bucks (tel: 0234 712266) (W, SQ)
Hewit & Son Ltd, Unit 28, Park Royal Metro Centre, Britannia Way, off Coronation Road, London NW10 7PR (tel: 081 965 5377) (M, SQ, LQ)

Pure silks
C.I. Davis & Co. Ltd, 94–96 Seymour Place, London W1H 5DG (tel: 071 723 0895) (W, R)

Cotton, linen and canvas
Russell & Chapple Ltd, 23 Monmouth Street, London WC2 9DE (tel: 071 836 7521) (R)

Saddle linen
Ackland & Clark & Co. Ltd, 107 Ashley Road, Bristol BS6 (tel: 0272 556096) (W, SQ)

METAL FITTINGS

General
A.T.H. Alden Ltd, Unit A, Sutherland Road, London E17 6BU (tel: 081 531 3358) (W, LQ)

Buckles, press-studs, D-rings, screw studs
See General Suppliers

Locks
Liston Products (Bridgetown) Ltd, Unit 4, Union Street, Bridgetown, Cannock, Staffs (tel: 054 35 78565 (M, SQ)

Rivets
Rivet Supply Co. Ltd, Power Road, Chiswick, London W4 5PP (tel: 071 994 6238) (W)

REINFORCEMENTS

Grey board
Hewit & Son Ltd, Unit 29, Park Royal Metro Centre, Britannia Way, off Coronation Road, London NW10 7PR (tel: 081 965 5377) (SQ)

Viledon
Freudenberg Ltd, Lutterworth, Leicestershire LE17 4DU (tel: 0455 553081) (W)

TOOLS

Joseph Dixon Tool Co. Ltd, Bott Lane, Walsall, West Midlands (tel: 0922 220551) (M, SQ)

See also General Suppliers

Bench-mounted paring machines
James Brockman, High Ridge, Ladder Hill, Wheatley, Oxfordshire OX33 1HY (tel: 0865 875279 (M)

Sharpening stones
Toolmail (GMC) Ltd, 170 High Street, Lewes, East Sussex BN7 1YE (tel: 0273 477009) (R)

EUROPE

GENERAL SUPPLIERS

The Bear Gallery, Gabelsbergerstrasse 7, Eingang Turkenstrasse 80333, Munchen, Germany (tel: 089 280 03 33)

Laeder & Skind Special, Vandkunsten 3, 1467 Kobenhavn K, Denmark

LEATHER

Costil Tanneries de France, BP 35, 67380 Lingolsheim, France (tel: 88 78 72 12) (M)

Fortier-Beaulieu, BP146, 51 Rue Bellevue, 42308 Roanne, France (M) (tel: 77 72 35 99)

Masure Dhalluin SA, 140 Rue des Tanneurs, Estaimbourg, Belgium 7731 (tel: 069 35 25 75)

METAL FITTINGS

A.B.C. Morini sri, Via il Prato 73/75R, 50123 Firenze, Italy (tel: 055/219423–293030)

Amiet AG, CH–4515 Oberdorf, Switzerland (tel: 065–22 66 44) (M)

M.M.C. di A. Colombo & Co. snc, Via Aquilegi 27, 21100 Varese, Italy (tel: 0332/333801)

Neeb & Kuhn, 8781 Mittelsinn/Ufr, Germany (tel: 09356 5284) (M)
S. Poursin, 35 Rue de Vinaigriers, 75010 Paris, France (tel: 1 46 07 17 07)

TOOLS

Soubeyran Chavanne & Cie ('Blanchard'), Romilly-sur-Andelle, Rouen, France (M, SQ)

USA

DYES AND FINISHES

Dyo Chemical Co., PO Box 15771, Dallas, Texas 75215 (M)

Fiebing Chemical Co., 516 South Second Street, Milwaukee, Wisconsin 53204

Pliantine and PVA cement
Conservation Resources International Inc, 8000-H Forbes Place, Springfield, Virginia 22151 (tel: 703 321 7730)

GENERAL SUPPLIERS

Berman Leathercraft, 25LJ Melcher Street, Boston, Massachusetts 02210–1599 (tel: 617 426 0870)

Drake Leather Co. Inc., 3500 West Beverly Boulevard, Montebello, California 90640 (tel: 213 721 6370)

Flannagan Saddlery Hardware Corp., 370 Mclean Avenue, Yonkers, New York 10705 (tel: 914 968 9200)

Mid-Continent Leather, PO Box 4691, Tulsa, Oklahoma 74159

S-T Leather Co., PO Box 78188, 17th and Papin, St Louis, Missouri 63178

Tandy leather Co., PO Box 2934, Forth Worth, Texas 76113

Veteran Leather Co., 204 25th Street, Brooklyn, New York 11232 9970 (tel: 718 768 0300)

Weaver Leather Inc, P.O. Box 68, 7540 C.R. 201, Mt Hope, Ohio 44660 (tel: 216 674 1782)

Zack White Leather Co., 1515 Main Street, PO Box 315, Ramseur, North Carolina 2736 (tel: 919 824 4488)

LEATHER

Coral Leathers, Ebinger Bros Leather Co. Inc., 1 Peatfield Street, Ipswich, Massachusetts 01928

Hallmark Leather, 512 Industrial Avenue, East Greensboro, North Carolina (tel: 919 272 4559)

Horween Leather Co., 2015 Elston Avenue, Chicago, Illinois 60614

Marap Leather Import & Export Co. Inc., 678 Broadway, New York 10012 (tel: 212 674 0078)

W. Pearce & Bros. Inc., 38 West 32nd Street, Dept C.M., New York 10001 (tel: 212 244 4559)

See also General Suppliers

METAL FITTINGS

The Partrade Company, 3888 East 45th Avenue, Suite 310, Denver, Colorado 80216 (tel: 303 399 4623)

Waterbury Buckle Co., 952 South Main Street, Westbury, Connecticut 06721 (M)

See also General Suppliers

TOOLS

Campbell Bosworth Machinery Co., 720 North Flagler Drive, Fort Lauderdale, Florida 33404 (tel:305 463 7910)

Gomph-Hackbarth Tools, RR#1, Box 7-B, Elfrida, Arizona 85610 (tel: 602 642 3891)

C.S. Osborne Tool Co., 137 Jersey Street, Harrison, New Jersey 07029 (tel: 201 483 3232) (M)

Tandy Leather Co., PO Box 2934, Fort Worth, Texas 76113

SHARPENING STONES

Woodcraft Supply, 210 Wood County Industrial Park, PO Box 1686, Parkersbury, West Virginia 26102

AUSTRALIA AND NEW ZEALAND

For up-to-date information about suppliers in these countries write to the leather guilds and craft associations listed under Useful Addresses on page 120.

GENERAL SUPPLIERS

E. Astley & Sons Ltd, 44 Portage Road, New Lynn, Auckland, New Zealand (tel: Auckland 875 759)

Colourite Leather Service Ltd, 62 Ben Lomond Crescent, Pakuranga, Auckland, New Zealand (tel: 09 568 066)

Tasmin Tanning Co. Ltd, PO Box 217 Wanganui, New Zealand

USEFUL ADDRESSES

UK

Association of Designer Leatherworkers, c/o 37 Silver Street, Tetbury, Gloucestershire

British Leather Confederation, The Leather Technology Centre, Leather Trades House, Moulton Park, Northampton (tel: 0604 494131)

Crafts Council, 44a Pentonville Road, Islington, London N1 9HF (tel: 071 278 7700)

Leather Conservation Centre, 34 Guildhall Road, Northampton NN1 1EW (tel: 0604 232 723)

Rural Development Commission, 141 Castle Street, Salisbury, Wiltshire (tel: 0722 6255)

Society of Designer Bookbinders, 6 Queen Square, London WC1N 3AR

Society of Designer Craftsmen, 24 Rivington Street, London EC2 (tel: 071 739 3663)

Welsh Arts Council, Craft and Design Department, Museum Place, Cardiff

REPUBLIC OF IRELAND

Crafts Council of Ireland, Powers Court, Town House Centre, South William Street, Dublin 2 (tel: 0001 353 1679 7368)

EUROPE

Promotions des Exportations de la Tannerie Française, 122 rue de Provence, Paris, France

Unione Nazionale Industria Conciara, Via Brisa 3–21023, Milan, Italy

USA AND CANADA

American Crafts Council, 72 Spring Street, New York, NY 10012, USA (tel: 0101 212 274 0630)

Canadian Crafts Council, 189 Laurier Avenue East, Ottawa, Ontario, Canada K1 N6P1

Canadian Society of Creative Leathercraft, 1357 Baldwin Street, Burlington, Ontario

Honourable Cordwainers Company, 106 Indian Summer Lane, Williamsburg, Virginia 23188 (tel: 804 565 6440)

International Federation of Leather Guilds, PO Box 102, Arcadia, Indiana 46030

The Luggage, Leathergoods, Handbags and Accessories Association of Canada, 2330 Bridletowne Circle Suite 2112, Scarborough, Ontario, Canada M1W 3P6 (tel: 416 491 5844)

Ontario Crafts Council, 35 McCaul Street, Toronto, Ontario M5T 1V7

Rawhide & Leather Braiders Association, 2842 North US 441 Belle Glade, Florida 33430

AUSTRALIA AND NEW ZEALAND

Association of New Zealand Leatherworkers, 44 Clifton Road, Takapuna, Auckland 9

Australian Plaiters & Whipmakers Association, PO Box 274, Kurando, Queensland 4872

Crafts Council of Australia, 100 George Street, The Rocks, Sydney, New South Wales (tel: 02 241 1701)

Crafts Council of New Zealand, First Floor, James Cook Arcade, Lampton Quay, Wellington (tel: 727 018)

Leathercrafters Association of Queensland, 2 Rutherford Street, Stafford, Queensland 4053

Leatherworkers Guild of New South Wales, 3 Bimbadean Street, Epping, New South Wales 2121

Leatherworkers Guild of South Australia, PO Box 370, Campbelltown 5074, South Australia

COURSES

UK

Cordwainers College, 182 Mare Street, London E8 3RE (tel: 081 985 0273) Full-time courses on making and designing leather goods, footwear and saddlery.

Valerie Michael, 37 Silver Street, Tetbury, Gloucestershire GL8 8DL (tel: 0666 502179) Two- and three-day weekend courses based on this book.

Rural Development Commission, 141 Castle Street, Salisbury, Wiltshire (tel: 0722 336255) Five-day courses to develop skills in saddle, harness and collar making; also leather vessels, bellows and gig saddles.

Walsall College of Art, Leather Goods Training Centre, 56/57 Wisemore, Walsall (tel: 0922 721153) Full-time, two-year BTEC national diploma course in Light Leather Goods Design.

West Dean College, West Dean, Chichester, West Sussex PO18 0QZ (tel: 0243 63 301) Specialists in long and short courses in most areas of arts and crafts; three- and five-day leather courses with Valerie Michael.

REPUBLIC OF IRELAND

For details of institutions offering courses in leatherworking, contact:

The Crafts Council of Ireland, Powers Court, Town House Centre, South William Street, Dublin 2 (tel: 0001 353 1679 7268)

EUROPE

Centro di Formazione Professionale, Via degli Stagnacci Bassi, 18/20 50010 Badia a Settimo, Firenze, Italy (tel: 0039–55 73.10.301).

Il Centro di Formazione Professionale "La Strada", Via o Salomone, 23-c/o Parrochia San Galdino-20138 Milan, Italy (tel: 02/50.63.982).

Sarteco, Via Verdi, 40 – 50053 Empoli / FI, Italy (tel: 0039 72444).

USA AND CANADA

For details of institutions offering courses in leatherworking, contact:

American Crafts Council, 72 Spring Street, New York, NY 10012, USA (tel: 0101 212 274 0630).

Canadian Crafts Council, 189 Laudier Avenue East, Ottawa, Ontario, Canada K1 N6P1.

AUSTRALIA

Canberra School of Art, PO Box 804, Canberra, ACT 2601 (tel: 06 249 5722) BA course in leather.

MUSEUMS TO VISIT

UK

Museum of Leathercraft, Central Museum, Guildhall Road, Northampton (tel: 0604 34881). Large historic and contemporary collection. Open from Monday to Saturday. Very good library for use by appointment only.

Northampton Shoe Museum, Central Museum, Guildhall Road, Northampton (tel: 0604 34881). Probably the largest shoe collection in the world. Open daily.

Street Shoe Museum, C. & J. Clark Ltd, Street, Somerset (tel: 0458 43131). Good collection of shoes and machinery.

Walsall Leather Centre Museum, 56–57 Wisemore, Walsall WS2 8EQ (tel: 0922 721153). A lively museum with historical displays and workshops. Developing a contemporary collection. Good library and helpful staff. Open daily.

EUROPE

Bibliothèque Communale de Stavelot, Stavelot, Belgium

Deutsches Ledermuseum/Schumuseum, Frankfurter Strasse 86, 605 Offenbach am Main, Germany (tel: 0611 81 30 21). A large international historical collection. Illustrated catalogue and other books produced by the museum. Open daily.

Hermes, 24 Fauberg St Honoré, 75008 Paris, France (tel: 40 17 47 77). A museum dedicated to the horse and means of travel, housed over Hermes' shop and workshops. Ask for details of a new museum of 'Hermes Creations' situated in another part of Paris.

Hungarian National Museum, Budapest, Hungary. Has some unuusal examples of Turko-Hungarian leatherwork.

Maison de la Peau et du Gant de Millau, Hotel Pegayrolles, Place Foch, 12100 Millau, France (tel: 65 59 01 08)

Musée du Cuir et de la Tannerie, BP 10, 37110, Château-Renault, France

Musée de la Vie Wallonne, Liege, Belgium

Museo de la Piel, Igualada, Carretera de Manresa 65, Barcelona, Spain. The main Spanish leather museum.

Nederlands Leder & Schoenen Museum, Elzenweg 25, 5144 MB Waalwijk, Holland

Palacio de Viana, Plaza don Gome, Cordoba, Spain (tel: 25 04 14). Leather wall hangings and furniture.

Posada del Potro, Plaza del Potra, Cordoba, Spain. A restored Arab inn housing a collection of Cordoban leatherwork and wall hangings dating from the fifteenth century.

Shoe Museum, Corso Carour, Vigevano, Lombardy, Italy. Italy's only shoe museum. Open Sundays only.

USA

Gene Autry Western Heritage Museum, Pine Meadows, Griffith Park, Los Angeles. Large collection of saddles and horse equipment.

Colonial Williamsburg, Williamsburg, Virginia. A living history museum, including shoe and harness making workshops.

Coach Leather Factory, 516 West 134th Street, 10th Avenue, New York (tel: 594 1850). A private collection that can be seen by appointment only.

JAPAN

Negishi Equine Museum, 1–3 Negishidai, Naka-Ku, Yokohama-S, Kanagawa 231

FURTHER READING

Books about leather generally fall into one or more of the following categories: instructional – how to work with leather (I); historical – leather and its uses throughout history (H); technical – how leather is made (T); and inspirational – examples of the creative use of leather (In). Sadly, most of the books listed below are no longer in print, but it should be possible to obtain access to them through the public library service or through a good museum library. In addition to the above abbreviations, those books that are recommended reading are marked with an asterisk (*) or, if they are highly recommended, with two asterisks (**). Titles that were in print at the time of writing this book are indicated by the abbreviation (IP), and those that explain decorative techniques are indicated by (D).

Adcock, K.J., *Leather*, Pitman Publishing, London, 1915

Attwater, W.A., *The Technique of Leathercraft*, B.T. Batsford, London, 1983 (I)*

Cherry, R., Leathercrafting: *Procedures and Projects*, Tandy Leather Co., Texas (IP, D)

De Recy, G., *The Decoration of Leather*, Constable, London, 1905 (I, H, D)*

Double, W.C., *Design and Construction of Handbags, trade text book, 1960 (I)*

The Fibre Structure of Leather, Leather Conservation Centre, Northampton (T, IP)

Foster, W., *Bags and Purses*, B.T. Batsford, London, 1985, (H, IP)

Freidrich, R., *Cuir – Tradition, Creation*, Dessain et Tolra, 1986 (I, IP)

Garbett, G. and Skellan, I., *The Wreck of the Metta Catharina*, New Pages, 1989 (Book about a ship that sank in 1786 with its cargo of 'Russia' leather; the wreck has been found and the leather can be bought . . . at a price; book and leather from The Cottage, Pulla Cross, Truro, Cornwall, UK)

Grant, B., *Encyclopedia of Rawhide and Leather Braiding*, Cornell Maritime Press, 1972 (I, IP)

Hamilton-Head, I., *Leatherwork*, Blandford, Poole, 1983 (I)

Hartley-Edwards, E., *The Country Life Book of Saddlery*, Country Life, London, 1981 (H, IP)

Hasluck, P., *Saddlery and Harness Making*, Cassell, London, 1904 (I)

John W. Waterer: Leather in Life, Art and Industry (biography and catalogue of an exhibition celebrating the centenary of his birth), Museum of Leathercraft, Northampton, 1992 (H, IP)**

Lingwood, R., *Leather in Three Dimensions*, Van Nostrand Reinhold, London, 1980 (Available from the author SRR #1, Bright, Ontario, Canada N0J 1B0) (I, In)*

MacGregor, N. & Michael, V., *Leather Resources III*, 1993 (Comprehensive listing of suppliers useful to small workshops; available from 37 Silver Street, Tetbury, Gloucestershire, UK)**

Moseley, G.C., *Leather Goods Manufacture*, Pitman Publishing, London, 1945; reprinted by Walsall Leather Centre Museum, 1992 (I, IP)**

Salaman, R.A., *Dictionary of Leatherworking* Tools, Unwin Hyman Ltd, London, 1985 (H, I)**

Shoes, Fashion and Fantasy, Thames & Hudson, London, 1989 (In, H, IP)

Smith, P., *The Book: Art and Object* 1982 (Available from Philip Smith, The Book House, Yatton Keynell, Chippenham, Wiltshire, UK) (In, IP)*

Stohlman, A., *How to Carve Leather*. (D) (IP) One of a large range of books written by him and available from Tandy Leather Co., PO Box 2934, Fort Worth, Texas 76113, USA

Swann, J., *Shoes*, B.T. Batsford, London, 1982 (H, IP)

Tylden, C., *Discovering Harness and Saddlery*, Shire Publications Ltd, Princes Risborough, 1979 (IP)

Waterer, J.W., *Leather in Life, Art and Industry*, Faber & Faber, London, 1946 (H, T)*

Waterer, J.W., *Leather and Craftsmanship*, Faber & Faber, London, 1950 (H)*

Waterer, J.W., *Leather Craftsmanship*, Bell & Hyman, London, 1968 (H, I)*

Waterer, J.W., *Leather and the Warrior*, Museum of Leathercraft, Northampton, 1981 (Available from J. Meade, 3 Oxbourne Cottages, Mill Lane, Shoreham, Kent, UK) (H, IP)*

Waterer, J.W., *Spanish Leather*, Faber & Faber, London, 1971, (H)*

Waterer, J.W., *John Waterer's Guide to Leather Conservation*, Museum of Leathercraft, Northampton, 1972 (I, T, IP)

Wilcox, D. and Manning, J., *Leather*, Pitman Publishing, London, 1974 (I, In)

PERIODICALS

Arpel, Via Ippolito Nievo, 33–20145 Milan, Italy (tel: 02 315951)

Fashion Extras, 86 Clarendon Road, West Croydon, Surrey CR0 3SG, UK

The Harness Shop News, PO Box 758 Cullowhee, North Carolina 28723, USA

Leather (international journal of the leather industry), Benn Publications, Sovereign Way, Tonbridge, Kent, UK

Leather Artisan, ANZL, 44 Clifton Road, Takapuna, Auckland 9, New Zealand

Leather Crafters Journal, 4307 Oak Drive, Rhinelander, Wisconsin 54501, USA

Luggage and Leathergoods News, c/o The Luggage, Leathergoods, Handbags and Accessories Association of Canada, 2330 Bridletowne Circle Suite 1221, Scarborough, Ontario, Canada M1W 3P6 (tel: 416 491 5884)

INDEX

Page numbers in *italic* refer to illustrations.

Acrylic dyes and paints 31–2, 84
Adhesives 23–4, 44, 117
Advanced projects 96–115
Airbrush 32
Attaché cases 52
    flat handles for 71
    lock for 26
Awl 14–15
    handles 15
    scratch 15, 29, 63
    stitching 46–50, *53*, 65
    stitching handles 71
    to set blade 20, *21*

Back of hide 12, 30, 68
Back stitching 55–6
Bags
    box stitch 52–4
    buckles 64
    with D-ring and screw stud 66
    design for shoulder bag 28–9
    gluing turned edges 44
    gusset 42–3, 58
    handles 70–1
    moulded *73*, 76
    moulded shoulder 100–5
    pockets for lined 60
    project for box bag 96–9
    project, large shoulder 110–15
    quilted calf *38*
    right-angled bends 43
    straps for 68–70
    thickness of hide 12
    turned edge 41
Beeswax 23, 46, 47
Beginners' projects 78–85
Belly area 12, 29, 73
Belts
    buckles 64–5
    gluing 44
    hide for 30
    lined calf 44
    paring for 40
    project for hide belt 78–*80*
    project for quilted belt 106–9
    stitching in belt loop 79
    thickness of hide 12

Bench vice 26, 66
Bevelling
    edge 15, 20, 34, *35*
    gusset top 59
    handles 71
    shoulder straps 68–9
Billet 64, 68, 105
Binding an edge *see* Bound edge
Bindings, paring for 40
Block
    for bags and purses 52
    for box 53
    for box bag 96
Bone folder
    bookbinder's 15
    gussets 58, 59
    hand stitching 46
    pockets 60
Bookbinder's hammer 16
Bookbinding suppliers 117
Boots 54
Bound-edge 34, 37–8, 42, 45
Box bag, project 96–9
Box stitch 46, 52–4, 55
Boxes
    hide *52*
    moulding 72
    right-angled bends 43
    square 53–4
    thickness of hide 12
Bridle makers 55
Brief case
    flat handles for 71
    lock for 26
    project for small 92–5, *95*
British Museum Leather Dressing 24
Buckets 54
Buckles 64–5
    for belt project 78
    leather-covered 64–5, 108
    metal 25–6
    paring for 40
    for straps 68–9
Buffed surface 12, 31
Bulldog clips 15
    leather-covered 44, *65*
Burnisher 15

Burnishing
    edge 34–6
    edge of buckles 65
    gusset top 59
    handles 71
    pockets 60
    shoulder straps 68–9
    surface 32–3
Butt area 12, 29, 30, 68
Butt stitching 46, 54–5, 70

Calf
    French binding 38
    piped seam 39
    pockets 60
    purses 81
    straps 70
Canvas for edge burnishing 34
Carving 75
Case hardening 11
Cases
    box stitch 52
    channelling 43
    flat pocket for 60
    gussets 58
    handles for 70–1
    locks for 62–3
    screw studs 66
    straps for 68–70
    thickness of hide 12
    see also Attaché and Brief-case
Casting stitches 50–1, 53
Cements 23
Channelling 43
Channels
    for gussets 59
    for square box 53
Chrome tanning 10–11, 60
Clamp 15, 46, 47
Cleaning 32
Clicking knives 17
Collar boxes 54
Combination oil stone 19, 26
Compass race 43, 58, 59
Compass/dividers 15
Contact adhesive 44
Cord for handles 70

Core diameters 70
Cork block 54, 59, 70
Corner stitching 52–4
Courses 121
Cow hide 12–13 see also Hide
Creaser 15
Creasing 36
    gussets 59
    straps 68–9
Crew punch 17, *105*
Currier 31, 32
Cut-edge
    finishing 34–6
    finishing for straps 70
    flat pockets 60
Cutting 29–30
Cutting-board 15

D-rings 26
    buckles 64
    flat handles 71
    gussets and 58
    holders 40, 66, 69–70
    paring for 40
    screw studs and 66
    straps 68–9
Decoration 75–6
Design for shoulder bag 28–9
Designing 28–30, 68
Dividers 15, 36, 46, 63
Doming punches 26, 62
Dressings 23–4, 31–2
Drinking vessels 72
Durable dots (studs) 26, 66, 81–2
Dye bench 32
Dyeing 31–3, *35*
Dyes 23
    suppliers of 117, 118

Edge beveller 15
    sharpening 20
Edge fiinishing 34–9
    bevelling 34, 35
    burnishing 34–6
    creasing 36
    cut edge 34
    dyeing *35*
    edge beveller 34, *35*
    edge shaves 34
    fine edge 40–2
    straps 69–70
    turned edge 41
    type of 34
Edge shave 15
Elastic bands 54

Embosser 75
Emery paper and cloth 26
Essential hand tools 14, 15
Extractor fan 32

Fabric 55
Fat liquor 32
Feeding leather 23, 32
Fiebing's 4-Way Care 31
Files 26
    rat's tail 62
Fine edge 40–2
Finishing 31–9
Flaps, screw studs for 66
Flat handles 71
    pockets 60–1
Flat-backed metal snips 26
Folding-top bag 90–2, *86*
Folio lock 26
Forming 74
Free-form moulding 73
French binding 38
Full grain 12

G-cramps 16, 59, *103*
Glazed surface 32
Glues 23
Gluing 44–5
Goat 39
Gouging *see* channelling
Grain shoulders 29
Greaseproof paper 45
Grey board 24
Gum 24
Gussets 42–3, 57–9
    box stitched 96–9
    gluing 44
    gussetted pockets 60
    pleated 60
    three-piece *57*, 58–9, 94
    u-shaped *57*, 59, 112–4

Hacksaw blade 17, 26
Half-buckles 64
Hammer
    bookbinder's 16
    hide 16, 46, 75
    metal 26, 62
    shoemaker's 16
    wooden 16
Hand stitching 14, 46–56
    see also stitching
Handles 70–1
    flat 71
    paring for 40

round 70–1
    small brief-case 94
Hanging pockets 60–1
Harness 64
Harness makers 43
Harness needles 17, 46, 47
Hasp of locks 62
Heat for moulding 73
Helmets 54, 72
Hide 29–30
    belt, project 78–80
    belts 30, 64
    belts and straps 40, 68
    hammer 16, 46, 75
    mallet 67
Holder, buckle 64

Incising lines 75
Intermediate projects 86–95
Invisible closure 67

Japanese water stone 19
Jewellery case, lock for 26

Keeper for straps 69
Kid 38
Knives 16–17
    ckicking 17
    paring 17, 40, 41
    sharpening 19, 20
    shoemaker's 16
    stitching 46
    swivel 75

Lacquer 31
Large shoulder bag, project 110–15
Lasting of shoes 74
Lead block 62
Leather
    buckles 64–5, 108
    bulldog clips 44, 65
    character and structure 10
    finishing 32–3
    linings 45
    suppliers 117
    thickness conversion chart 12
Linen thread 22, 46, 65
Linings
    fabric 45
    gluing 44, *45*
    for gussets 59
    linen 113
    magnetic studs and leather 67
    for straps 70
    suppliers 117, 118

Litho stone 34, 40, 41
Locking needles on to thread 47
Locks 25–6, 62–3
    attaching 63
Loop, belt 79
    straps 69
Losing a stitch 55, *99*, 98

Magnetic studs 26, 67, 87, *88*
Mallet, hide or wooden 67
Marble 40, 75–6
Masks 29, *83*
    free-form moulding 73
    project 83–5
    thickness of hide 12
    tooling 75–6
Materials 22–4
    for box bag 96
    for folding-top bag 90
    for hide belt 78
    for large shoulder bag 110
    for mask 83
    for moulded shoulder bag 100–1
    for purse 81
    for quilted belt 106
    for small brief-case 92–3
    for wallet and passport holder 87
Metal fittings 25–6, 62, 117–19
Metal hammer 26, 62
Metal polish 26
Metal rule 19, 43, 58, 68
Metal snips 62
Modellers 75–6
Mould
    for buckles 65
    for gussets 59
    for purse 74
    for round box 54
    for shoulder bag 100
Moulded purse 72
Moulded shoulder bag 100–5
Moulding 72–5
    masks 29, 84
    one-piece 74–5
    shaped bag 76
    for shoulder bag 102–4
    thickness of hide 12
    three-piece 73–4
    two-piece 74

Nails for moulds 75
Neatlac 31
Needles 17
    harness 46
    locking on to thread 47

Oil stone, combination 19, 26
Oiling 32
One-piece cut-edged gusset 58
One-piece moulds 74–5
Oven for moulds 73
Oxalic acid 32

Paring
    knife 17, 20, 40, *41*, 42
    machine *18*, 40, 41, *42*, 64
    pockets 60
    or skiving 40–2, 64, 68–9
    stone *18*, 40, *41*
Passport holder and wallet 86–9
Pattern making 28–30
Pigskin 60, 70, 81
Pin vice 26
Piped seams 39
Pistol holders 72
Pleated gusset pockets 60
Pliantene 24, 31, 33 *see also* British
    Museum Leather Dressing
Pliers *18*, 19, 42, 46
Plough gauge *18*, 30, 68
Plywood for moulds 74
Pockets 60–1
    for brief-case 94
    flat and hanging 60–1, *113*, 94
    gluing 44
    for large shoulder bag 112–13
for moulded bag 105
    pleated *112*
    tops 41
    wallet and passport holder 88
Polishes 23–4, 31
    metal 26
Polishing 32
Press 18
Press-studs 26, 66
Pricking iron *18*, 46, *47*, 53–5, 59, 70
Pricking wheel 19, 47, 65
Projects 77–114
    advanced 96–115
    beginners' 78–85
    box bag 96–9
    folding-top bag 90–2
    hide belt 78–80
    intermediate 86–95
    large shoulder bag 110–15
    mask 83–5
    moulded shoulder bag 100–5
    purse 81–2
    quilted belt 106–9
    small brief-case 92–5
    wallet, passport holder 86–9

Punches 19
    doming 26, 62
Purses 52
    project 80, 81–2
    three-piece moulds 73–4
    turned edge 41
PVA adhesive 44, 45, 65

Quilted bag *109*
Quilted belt 106–9
Quilted calf bag *38*
Quilting 46

Race (grooving tool) 19, 43, 53
Rat's tail file 62
Reinforcements 24
    gluing 44
    for straps 70
    suppliers 118
Repairs and back stitch 55
Revolving punch plier 19, 67
Rings 26 *see also* D-rings
Rivets *25*, 26, 62–3
Rope 70
Round box 54–6
Round handles 70–1
Rounding 70–1, 69
Rubber solution 24, 44, 53, *55*
Ruler 19, 43, 58, 68
Russet (pre-dyed) 12, 73

Saddle soap 24, 31
Saddle stitch 46–51, 53, 70–1
Saddlers 43, 55
Saddlery buckles 25
Sam Browne studs 67
Sandpaper, washers and 63
Scissors 19
Scratch awl 15, 29, 63
Screw crease 36
Screw studs 26, 66, 91, 98
Scriber 26
Sculptures 72
Shaping wet leather 72–5
Sharpen, to
    edge bevellers 20
    knives 19, 20
Sharpening stone 19, 118, 119
Shields 72
Shoe cream, neutral 24, 31, 33
Shoemaker's hammer 16
Shoemaker's knife 16
Shoes 54
    shaping uppers 74
Shoulder bag

design brief for 28–9
project for box-stitched 96–9
project for folding top 90–2
project for large 110–15
project for moulded 100–5
Shoulders
  for belts or straps 30, 68
  grain 29
  of hide 12, 68
Side of hide 12, 30
Side-pleated pocket *61*
Silk thread 22, 108
Single buckles 64
Single crease 36
Single race 43
Skins
  characteristics and types 13
  cutting 30
  paring 40
  straps 70
  turned edge 41
Skiving or paring 40–2, 64, 68–9
Snips, flat-backed metal 26, 62
Spirit lamp 19
Spirit-based dyes 23, 31–2
Split or round closing 54
Splitting leather, for gussets 58
Splitting machine 19, 42–3
Stamping 75–6
Stamps for tooling 75
Stiffener 70
Stitching
  awl for 14–15
  back 55–6
  box 46, 52–4
  butt 46, 54–5, 70
  casting 50–1
  channels for decorative 43
  corner 52–4
  hand 46–56
  locking needle on to thread 47
  losing a stitch 55, *99*
  quilting 46
  saddle 46–51, 53, 70
  tools and materials 46

Stones
  combination oil 19, 26
  litho 34, 40, 41
  paring 18
  sharpening 19
    suppliers of 118–19
Straight-edge, metal 19, 43, 58
Straps 30, 58, 68–70
  bag 68–70
  buckles 64–9
  lining 70
  paring for 40
  screw studs for 66
  shoulder 68–70
  skin 70
Strop 19, 40
Studs 26, 58, 66–7, 91, 98
Suppliers 117–19
Surface decoration 75–6
Swivel knife 75
Sword scabbards 54

Tan hide, brief-case *95*
Tanning 10–12
Textured effects 75
Thickness conversion chart 12
Thread 22
  lined 22, 46, 65
  locking needles on to *47*
  silk 22
  suppliers 118
Three-piece cut-edged gusset 58–9
Three-piece gussets 60
Three-piece moulds 73–4
Tooling 75–6
Tools 14–21
  for box bag 96
  for decorating *75*
  essential 14, *16*
  for folding-top bag 90
  for hide belt 78
  for large shoulder bag 110
  for mask 83
  for moulded shoulder bag 100–1
  for preparing metal fittings *26*

for purse 81
for quilted belt 106
for small brief-case 93
suppliers 118, 119
useful 17
for wallet and passport holder 87
Tracers 75
Turn-locks 26
Turned edge 37, 41
  binding for gussets 59
  gluing 44, 45
  paring for 40
  pockets 60
  or turned-edge binding 34, 37
Turning allowance 59, 70
Turning pattern for gussets 59
Turnover 41
  binding 38
Twist 22
Two-piece moulds 74

U-shaped bound-edge gusset *57*, 59
U-shaped cut-edged gusset 59

Vegetable tanning 11–12, 31, 60, 72,
  117
Vice, bench, pin and small 26, 66
Vileden 24

Wall hangings 72
Wallets
  gluing 44
  project, and passport holder 86–9
  turned edge 41
Washer, leather 63, 67
Water-based dyes 23, 31–2
Wet-mould 74–5
Wire wool 26
Wooden dowel 70
Wooden hammer 16
Wooden mallet 67
Wooden moulds 73–5
Writing cases 44